THE SINGLE SOURCE
OF ALL FILTH

By the Same Author

Classic Drama
The Drama and Theatre Arts Course Book
A Practical Guide to Drama in the Secondary School
Television Drama: An Introduction

A Consideration of the Opinions of
REVD JEREMY COLLIER, M.A.
on the English Stage

The Single Source
of
All Filth

Together with
The Views of his Defendants, Critics and the Dramatists

By DAVID SELF

J. Garnet Miller

Copyright © by David Self 2000

First published in the United Kingdom By J. Garnet Miller
(An imprint of Cressrelles Publishing Company Limited)
10 Station Road Industrial Estate, Colwall,
Malvern WR13 6RN

British Library Cataloguing-in-Publication Data
A CIP record for this book is available from the British Library

ISBN: 0 85343 626 6

Printed and bound in England by Polestar Scientifica, Exeter

Contents

Illustrations

Acknowledgements

First, and most importantly, I must acknowledge the help and encouragement I received many years ago as a student at Chester College when my tutor, Alan Bownas, suggested the Reverend Jeremy Collier to me as a possible subject for a thesis and subsequently supervised my work on him - work which has been incorporated, in part, within this book.

I also acknowledge with gratitude the help I have received from the staff of the Norfolk and Norwich Central Lending and Information and Reference Libraries. I am also much indebted for help with Chapter One to Ellie Clewlow (Archivist of Gonville and Caius College, Cambridge), David Warnes (Third Master and Historian of Ipswich School) and Mrs A. L. West (Suffolk Record Office).

Finally, my special thanks are due to Monica Dorrington for keying quotations from original sources.

The engraving of Jeremy Collier by J. Hopwood is reproduced by permission of the Hulton-Getty Picture Collection.

for Paul

Introduction

To say that Jeremy Collier was a clergyman of strong convictions is a magnificent understatement. He appears to have been blissfully free of self-doubt and to have lived his life in a white fury of indignation at those who failed to adopt his ecclesiastical and moral stances. He was, frankly, a bigot or, to put it in current, politically correct terms, a religious conservative and traditionalist. Like many such characters, unpopularity was no problem for Collier.

He aborted his own clerical career with his refusal to swear allegiance to William and Mary, following the removal of James II from the throne in 1688. That is, he became a Non-juror and therefore ineligible for any office in the Established Church of England. Eight years later, he also became an outlaw. When two men, Sir John Friend and Sir William Parkins, were to be executed for plotting the assassination of King William, Collier turned up and gave them absolution at the foot of the scaffold without hearing their confession, so "he knew not the state of their souls". It was for this that he was outlawed.

While on the run, he wrote his most famous publication, *A Short View of the Immorality and Profaneness of the English Stage* and published it in 1698. He defined his argument in the opening sentence:

> The business of plays is to recommend virtue and discountenance vice;
> to shew the uncertainty of humane greatness, the sudden turns of fate,
> and the unhappy conclusions of violence and injustice.

Despite proving he had little sense of humour and showing he was blindly incandescent with rage at the dramatists of his day, the *Short View* had an immediate effect. King William granted him a pardon. Within weeks Vanbrugh and Congreve replied in print and Collier responded with further pamphlets. In 1703, a London theatre was destroyed during a thunder storm. Collier again burst forth with a squeal of triumph in yet another pamphlet, and so breathed new life into the debate. In all, some forty wildly passionate books and pamphlets, together with an outrageously libellous play *The Stage Beaux Toss'd in a Blanket,* appeared between 1698 and 1725 as a direct result of the *Short View.*

The Restoration theatre was indeed notable for the robustness, even lewdness, of its comedy. There was ample room for criticism. Like a certain kind of modern Sunday tabloid, the dramatists professed to attack the manners and the values of the age yet came very close to celebrating their excesses. Even so, Collier's exaggerations should have devalued his criticisms. His inability to see a joke should have attracted only mirth. And as a member, albeit a leading one, of a suspect church faction, his moral argument might have been seen as flawed.

Yet his prolific and intemperate polemics struck a popular chord, winning the approval of the growing middle-classes. He strangled the theatrical careers of Vanbrugh and Congreve and, partly thanks to his efforts, the stage was indeed reformed. What is more, the effect of his outbursts was long-lasting. Some years after his death, but resulting from his crusade, a court official, the Lord Chamberlain, was appointed censor of the theatre. Until 1968, the English stage which Collier defined as "the single source of all filth" was censored by Lords Chamberlain who could, on occasion, easily match Collier with their lack of humour.

Possibly because his writings are repetitive, they have not been much studied. Indeed, it is not easy even to obtain them. The original publications are available only in the 'precious books' sections of a handful of academic libraries, while a series of facsimile reprints published in the United States of America circa 1973 is itself something of a rarity. There are two seminal works about Collier: *Comedy and Conscience After the Reformation* by J. Krutch (New York 1924) and a graduate dissertation, *The Jeremy Collier Stage Controversy 1698-1726* by Sister Rose Anthony (Milwaukee 1937) - but neither of these works is easy to obtain.

The purpose of this work, then, is twofold. First, it aims to outline the salient points made during the controversy. And secondly, because the original publications are not easily accessible, it is intended to be as much an anthology of those writings as a critical survey. However, because it is intended primarily as an introduction to Collier for the general reader and the student of the theatre rather than as a work of academic or literary scholarship, the orthography and punctuation of the original texts have been modernised: for example, in the use of capital letters and in the punctuation of speech. The wording has not been altered - therefore obsolete words such as "prophaneness" have been preferred to the modern *profanity*. Contractions such as "o'er" (for *over*) have been modernised, but the frequently used and distinctive "'tis" has been allowed to stand. A few words not in concise dictionaries have been glossed where they occur.

David Self
Norwich 1999

Figure 1: Jeremy Collier

1

Priest, Critic and Historian

Jeremy, properly Jeremiah, Collier was born at Stow-cum-Quy, some five miles east of Cambridge, on 23 September 1650. His father, also called Jeremiah and known as Jeremy, came from Yorkshire. He had been a student at Trinity College, Cambridge from 1636, taking his Bachelor of Arts in 1639 or 1640 and his Master of Arts in 1643. He then migrated to St John's College, where he is recorded as being a Fellow in 1644. He was a linguist of some considerable eminence, took holy orders and became a schoolteacher at Boston Grammar School in Lincolnshire. Jeremy's mother was born Elizabeth Smith and had grown up in a respected family in Stow-cum-Quy.

From 1649 until 1653 Jeremy senior was master (headmaster) of Aldenham School near Elstree in Hertfordshire. Some time after this, the family moved to Ipswich. Certainly, they were living there by 1663, for in June 1663 Jeremy's father accepted the post of master of Ipswich School, then an endowed grammar school. It was located in the centre of the town and housed in what had formerly been the Ipswich Blackfriars, a monastic building standing much as it had been at the time of the dissolution of the monasteries. It was sadly demolished later. Young Jeremy, by now 13, became a pupil in his father's school.

Jeremy the elder's short and stormy career at Ipswich School prefigures many of his son's battles. Within a very short period of his taking up office, a committee had to be appointed "to hear the difference between the master and usher" (deputy headmaster). The next day a new usher was appointed - round one to the new master. But by the following January, another committee had been appointed, basically to conduct weekly inspections of the school "to see the scholars' Latin" and "to do what they shall think fit for the improvement of the said school". Either the committee was critical of the master's methods and achievements or he did not take kindly to this interference, as notice was given in April that a new master would be appointed at Michaelmas (September). Matters came to a head somewhat earlier. On 24 May, the Assembly or governing body announced that "Mr Collier shall this week be discharged of being schoolmaster". The new usher was placed in temporary charge and received the master's salary. We do not know whether young Jeremy continued as a pupil at the school after his father's sudden departure, but the fact that Jeremy senior does not appear in *The Lists of Suffolk Clergy* suggests he never obtained a living in the area. Incidentally, the author of the *Short View* would be mortified to learn that drama is now a flourishing activity at his old school!

On 10 April 1669, young Jeremy entered Caius College, Cambridge as a sizar or poor scholar. Unlike scholarships which were awarded competitively for academic attainment, sizarships were given on grounds of financial need. His father's occupation was recorded as clerk (cleric) in the village of Papworth, to the west of Cambridge. Jeremy studied under the tutelage of John Ellyr and appears to have been an able and diligent student, receiving his BA in the academic year 1672-3. Three years later he took his MA.

Also in 1676, and following in his father's footsteps, he entered the church and was ordained deacon at Michaelmas by Dr Peter Gunning, Bishop of Ely, Cambridge being in the Ely diocese. Some biographers and reference books state he was ordained in 1673 but *The Biographical History of Gonville and Caius College* gives the date precisely as 24 September 1676. On 24 February in 1678 (or 1677 if one follows the calendar then in use in England where the new year did not begin until 25 March), he was priested by Bishop Compton of London. Collier seems to have made some useful connections by this stage of his life, for his first appointment was as chaplain to the Countess of Dorset at Knole House, near Sevenoaks in Kent. Knole was, and still is, one of the great baronial mansions of the country, having been given by Elizabeth I to her cousin, Thomas Sackville, who was Lord High Treasurer of England and a descendant of a wealthy family. He was created Earl of Dorset in 1604.

In 1677, his descendant, the fifth Earl died and his son Charles inherited the title and Knole. Collier's precise position when he arrived at the house is just one of many uncertainties about his life. In some sources he is said to have been personal chaplain to the Countess; in others chaplain to the Dowager Countess, but the fifth Earl's wife had, however, pre-deceased him. Whatever his responsibilities, it is interesting to speculate on how Collier regarded the new Earl and the extent to which his stay at Knole formulated his convictions and later censorious attitude towards the stage. From a pamphlet he was to publish some twenty years later, *Upon the Office of a Chaplain*, it is possible to deduce there was friction between chaplain and employer.

In his rowdy youth, the sixth Earl (at that time Lord Buckhurst) is recorded by the diarist Samuel Pepys as being in the habit of passing on his mistresses to the King. He had also been a great frequenter of London's two theatres and intimately associated with the infamous Nell Gwyn. Back in 1667, when Nell was sixteen and had been acting for two years, Pepys tells us that Lord Buckhurst (aged about 30) "hath got Nell away from the King's House [the King's Theatre, otherwise known simply as The Theatre or Drury Lane], and gives her £100 a year, so as she will act no more." The couple kept "merry house" at Epsom in Surrey where Pepys was a visitor. But these arrangements did not last long. By August that year, Nell was back in London and acting once again. Pepys now noted that "Nell is already left by my Lord Buckhurst, and that he makes sport of her, and swears she hath had all she could get of him." Nell did not become the King's mistress until the following January.

Within ten years of this episode, Buckhurst was Earl, master of Knole and married. Otherwise he seems to have changed little. One of his descendants, Vita Sackville-West, wrote in *Knole and the Sackvilles*, that he "furnished Knole with silver, and peopled it with poets and courtesans". He created the house's Poet's Parlour with its portraits of Dryden and D'Urfey who were later to be savaged by Collier. Also hanging in the house, as it still does, was a portrait of Nell Gwyn - presumably by now a happy memory in the Earl's mind. Whether her charms were on display at Knole when Collier was chaplain is not known.

Ironically, in the light of the Earl's past and Collier's future, the Earl was later to become Lord Chamberlain - the court official to be entrusted in the next century with the task of censoring the stage. This appointment came about because of the Earl's strong dislike of James II who succeeded to the throne in 1685. So strong was his dislike of the new King that he took an active part in bringing about the accession of King William. His reward was his appointment as Lord Chamberlain, a post he held until 1697.

Figure 1: Jeremy Collier

Collier's stay in these heady circles was predictably short. On 25 September 1679, he was inducted vicar of the tiny village of Ampton in Suffolk. His stay in Ampton seems to have been without note, though he is commemorated by a memorial plaque on the church wall. It reads:

Remember Jeremy Collier MA, Rector of this Parish 1679-1684 Divine, Historian, Controversialist, Outlaw, Non-juring Bishop
Born 23 September 1650, Buried at Old St Pancras,
London 26 April 1726
"He was in the full force of the words, a good man."
MACAULAY

Macaulay being T. B. Macaulay, author of the famous *History of England*. A small notice nearby states, somewhat plaintively, "Jeremy Collier is the only famous rector of Ampton."

The next that we hear of him, according to all the standard reference works, including *The Biographical History of Gonville and Caius College* and *The Dictionary of National Biography*, is his appointment as lecturer at Gray's Inn in London in 1685. However, that same notice in Ampton Church also notes "the librarian there tells me they have no record of him there." This was confirmed by a later librarian in 1997: "I have been unable to confirm from our records that Jeremy Collier was either a member or a Reader [lecturer] of the Inn. Furthermore, it seems he never held the office of Preacher to the Society."

Whatever the truth of the situation, any such appointment can have lasted only three years. When William of Orange was invited to come to England to defend "its basic liberties" against the Catholic King James II, James fled the country. Collier took an active part in the controversy that followed James's flight. Upon the accession of William in 1688, Collier refused to swear the oath of allegiance required from all clergymen and so "the public exercise of his function became impracticable". Collier was by no means alone in taking this stance.

When the Bishop of Salisbury, Dr Burnett, published an *Enquiry into the State Affairs*, Collier answered with his first publication, a twelve-page pamphlet *The Desertion Discussed in a Letter to a Country Gentleman*. Collier argued that the king "had sufficient grounds to make him apprehensive of danger, and that therefore it cannot be called an abdication". Collier's pamphlet gave those now in authority such offence that its author was imprisoned at Newgate for some time, though he was eventually discharged without being brought to trial.

The truth was that the Glorious Revolution of 1688 created acute problems for the Church of England. It had vehemently championed the principle of legitimate succession and the duty of unquestioning obedience. So was it possible to swear allegiance to your lawful king, while his predecessor was still alive? Hence the debate and subsequent split within its ranks. Those who sincerely felt that they could not take the oath became known as Non-jurors. With a splendidly Anglican compromise, they were subsequently deprived of their livings but not defrocked: they remained priests of the Church of England but without pay or authority.

Nor, as is so often the case in ecclesiastical politics, was it that simple. In his history of *English Church Life*, Wickham Legg divides those who became popularly known as Non-jurors into three main groups. These were, first, those who had taken the oath, thus retaining their benefices, but then preached against it. Secondly, there were those who refused to take the oath, but continued to worship within the Church of England, receiving Communion from priests who had taken the oath. The third group, and this included Collier, were those who felt they could not take the oath but who continued to act as independent Anglican priests, forming their own congregations and administering Anglican rites. Though there was no formalised non-juring doctrine, it was, in effect, a schism. The movement never had more than 20,000 followers but did, however, number eight bishops and four hundred priests among its numbers. Their leader was the Bishop of Bath and Wells, Bishop Ken.

Because the priests within the movement tended to belong to the high church party of the Church, they were labelled 'Romish'. Indeed, in his play *The Non-Juror*, the actor and theatre manager Colly Cibber wrote of his non-juring priest:

> 'Tis true, name to him but Rome or popery, he startles, as at a monster, but gild its grossest doctrines with the style of English Catholic, he swallows down the poison, like a cordial.

6

Under Collier's direction, members of the sect later attempted to formalise their position through an alignment and inter-communion with the Eastern Orthodox Church. The Archbishop of Canterbury thwarted this by writing to the Patriarch of Jerusalem informing him that they were not part of the Church of England. Wickham Legg is blunter. He states directly that the non-juring priests were heretical - a statement many Anglicans would have endorsed as the seventeenth century came to an end.

The act of non-juring was, without doubt, the turning point of Collier's life. From this time on, he appears to have lived permanently in London, without further salary or stipend from the Church, and as something of an outsider - spending his time writing pamphlets and essays. On 8 November 1692, he was again arrested and imprisoned, this time on grounds of conspiring to restore James II to the English throne. He had visited the isolated Romney Marsh on the Kent coast with another Non-juror, Newton. Because of its proximity to France, the Marsh was a well-known landing area for fugitives, smugglers and illegal immigrants. Letters were produced, supposedly written by Collier to James II's son, known as *The Pretender* (to the throne). The evidence was inconclusive and Collier was granted bail. He, however, had other ideas. Soon after his release he decided that, by agreeing to bail, he had been inconsistent. Accordingly, he visited the Lord Chief Justice and surrendered himself to imprisonment. This time, he was bailed out again by friends after a week in prison - a week he had used to write a pamphlet arguing his case. He produced two further pamphlets in the following months, including a very bitter and intemperate one entitled *Remarks on the London Gazette*.

The next time Collier came to prominence was in 1696. Two men, Sir John Friend and Sir William Parkyns, were to be executed at Tyburn for their part in the Assassination Plot against King William. Collier visited them in Newgate prison and then, on the day of their execution at Tyburn, he and two other clergymen publicly gave them absolution, without hearing their confession, so that "he knew not the state of their souls". There was a considerable outcry. Collier's companions were arrested and imprisoned in Newgate. Collier escaped. Refusing to give himself up as a criminal, he was consequently outlawed. He was certainly hunted for a time, but apparently was not hotly pursued. His ever useful, possibly influential friends helped him into hiding, either in London or in some of the greater houses where he was able to make use of their libraries. On 9 April, he published his *Defence of the Absolution*. The very next day the Archbishops of Canterbury and York and twelve bishops condemned his action as wrong and heretical.

During the next two years, he published several pamphlets under the less than imaginative pseudonym of J. Smith; and then, in 1697, the first volume of his essays. Many of these essays were in dialogue form and are on various ethical and social topics such as *Duelling* and *Lying*. One is the previously mentioned *On the Office of the Chaplain*. Presumably reflecting his experiences at Knole, this essay advocates the avoidance of servility on the part of a family chaplain, and of arrogance on the part of his patron. He published two further volumes of essays, the last appearing in 1709.

Then in April 1698 came the publication of *A Short View of the Immorality and Profaneness of the English Stage* - and with it came immediate fame and attention. Collier's selection of the theatre as the source of all the nation's moral ills was either a very clever or fortuitous stroke. In attacking the stage, he made no onslaught on the establishment. Quite the contrary. By so doing, he was aligning himself with both the Church and its moralists and the City, a newly powerful, middle-class power base critical of aristocratic foppery. William III, recognising the political importance of Collier's outburst, granted him an immediate Royal Pardon. Collier was no longer an outlaw. He could appear once again in public and, indeed, seems quite rapidly to have become something of a celebrity or personality. The story of the counter-attacks on Collier and his further responses and denunciations forms the main part of this book, but his later years (he was 47 when the *Short View* was published) were by no means exclusively devoted to his battle with the playwrights and their supporters.

He showed himself to be something of a historian in 1701, when he published Volumes I and II of his *Historical Dictionary*, which was based on Louis Moréri's *Le Grand Dictionnaire Historique* (published in France in 1674). Collier's work was pronounced inaccurate during the reign of Anne, having first been quite well-received. He produced a *Supplement* and an *Appendix* in 1705. His next historical work was his *Ecclesiastical History of Great Britain* (1708). A second volume covering the period from Henry VII to 1700 appeared six years later. This has generally been considered a far better and more accurate work than his secular history and, indeed, for some years was the standard work on the subject, despite its predictable high church bias. He also championed the church's right not to be controlled by the monarch - for example, defending Becket against Henry II. As George Sampson wrote when assessing Collier and this work in particular in *The Cambridge History of English Literature*: "He was one of those fearless, conscientious, fanatical heroes who assert their convictions at any cost."

Throughout the first decade of the eighteenth century, Collier enjoyed mixed and almost contradictory reputations as a puritanical and therefore, by implication, a low church or evangelical reformer of the nation's morals - and as a near-papistical, high churchman. Parallels can be drawn with those high Anglicans who, in the last decade of the twentieth century, have united with evangelical or biblical Christians in their opposition to women priests and a loosening of traditional moral standards. Not surprisingly, given his disputatious nature, Collier was always in the forefront of public discussion, frequently taking up his pen to renew his attack on the stage and to defend his earlier statements.

Many attempts were made during Anne's reign to persuade this moral hero to rejoin the mainstream Anglican church, but his non-juring scruples were now respected. Indeed, in his later years, more and more of his time was taken up by his activities as a Non-juror. By 1713, Bishop Hickes was the only surviving non-juring bishop and he decided to consecrate Collier and two other priests as bishops, to follow in his footsteps. The event was described by the first historian of the Non-jurors, Dr Thomas Brett, himself a non-juring priest. This quotation is taken from Henry Broxap's 1928 history, *The Later Non-jurors*:

> Jeremiah Collier, MA, was consecrated a Bishop of the Church of England on Ascension Day, 14th May 1713, by George Hickes, Archibald Campbell and James Gadderar in Dr Hickes's oratory in Ormonde Street,

London, in the presence of Henry Gandy and Thomas Stampe, presbyters, and Heneage, Earl of Winchilsea and Sir Thomas Lestrange, Bart. Samuel Hawes, MA, and Nathaniel Spinckes, MA, were both consecrated bishops at the same time by the same persons.

At the time of his consecration as bishop, illegal in the eyes of the mainstream Church, Collier was in charge of a small congregation which met in Broad Street, London, in a chapel which was described as being up two flights of stairs. The charge of what was presumably a small congregation appears to have afforded little scope for a man of Collier's standing and eminence.

When Bishop Hickes died two years later, Collier came to be regarded as leader or *primus* of the sect. For some reason, the other two new bishops consecrated with Collier were reticent or even secretive about their status. To quote Brett again:

Mr Collier was the only one who at that time acted as a Bishop amongst the Non-jurors, it being thought expedient that the others should conceal their character even from their own people.

Collier's position as leader of the Non-jurors was formalised in 1716, again according to Brett:

When we met at Mr Gandy's on 23rd July 1716 I, myself, made a proposal that, forasmuch as it was not then thought convenient that every man's character should be publicly known, it might be proper for us to choose one with the title of Primus, to whom the clergy might apply as there should be occasion and who might call us together, when it was proper for us to meet and consult on any emergency, and to preside at such meetings. Which proposal was received unanimously and without any opposition and Mr C. was desired to take the chair with that title which for some time he declined and would have put it on some other person and did not accept of it without much entreaty - he did not assume the name of Primus nor was it put upon him by his flatterers but fairly conferred on him by his colleagues, even without his own seeking.

This seems to have been a fairly rare example of Collier's modesty but he soon took the opportunity afforded by his new position to make clear his preference for the 1549 *Order of Holy Communion*, which is much closer to the Latin Rite than the 1662 *Book of Common Prayer*. During the resulting controversy among the remaining Non-jurors, he was accused of holding Romish views. He answered his critics as he had so often done before: he set out his argument in a pamphlet -

Reasons for Restoring some Prayers and Directions as They Stand in the Communion Service of the First English Reformed Liturgy. The next year, 1718, the Non-jurors new office or form of service for Holy Communion appeared in a service book which was almost certainly the work of Collier. It denied the Roman doctrine of trans-substantiation, the belief that the bread and wine become the body and blood of Christ, but otherwise followed much Roman usage.

Despite the original arguments for the existence of the Non-jurors now being largely irrelevant - both Kings James and William were dead - the Non-jurors nevertheless remained a distinct and separate sect. For the next seven years however, Collier again entered into correspondence with the Eastern Church with a view to establishing some sort of official link.

It is at this point that an intriguing reference to Collier occurs in the diary of Thomas Hearne (1678-1735) who has been described as a "looker-on" of the Non-jurors. His entry for 4 May 1725 describes a meeting with a Non-juror turned farmer:

> I saw Mr Richard Russell, MA, formerly of University College, afterwards preferred to a living in the country which he lost upon account of the oaths, and now drives a farm to support himself, his wife and four children. Mr Russell told me that Mr Jeremy Collier is very poor in his old age, having married an odd wife, mother of Mr Thomas Deacon . . .

This Thomas Deacon was a young and fervent Non-juror, ordained within the sect, possibly by Collier, in 1716. His mother, Mrs Cecilia Deacon, the widow of William Deacon - a sea-captain of Stepney - was as forceful as her new husband. According to the writings of another non-juring bishop of the period, Archibald Campbell, she not only ruled the now ailing Collier but sought to manage the Non-jurors. Writing of one particular issue, Campbell noted: "'Tis old Pope Joan who presses this and thinks to govern now." The historian, Brett, confirms this nickname: "Mrs Collier, to whom for her impertinence was given the name Pope Joan . . ."

By the end of 1725, Collier was not only old but very weak from repeated and violent attacks of the "stone", that is gall or kidney stones, and almost an invalid. He was still able to write, however. Earlier that year there had appeared his *Several Discourses Upon Practical Subjects* and, in the first months of the following year, *God Not the Author of Evil*. He also seems to have been living in some poverty. His last letter to Thomas Brett is dated 2 November 1725:

> I have a fit of distemper upon me and therefore cannot help but be exceedingly brief. If you have the money you were so kind to pick up for me in trade, be pleased to send it when convenience presents, for it will not come unseasonably to yours etc.

He died on 26 April 1726, aged 76, and was buried in the churchyard of Old St Pancras Church, London - the district in which he had spent much of his active and provocative life. There is nothing to mark the spot where he was laid and the church registers the burial simply: "1726 April 29th. Jeremiah Collier. Clerk." The looker-on Hearne wrote in his diary:

> Last Tuesday died at London the Rev. Jer. Collier, a man of excellent parts and learning, and great integrity being a Non-juror, and deprived of what he had at the time of the wicked revolution. He was a Cambridge man and ought therefore to be reckoned among the famous worthies of that university. He writ and published many books, some of which are about the stage, an historical and geographical dictionary, a church history of Britain, essays, etc.

His death was also the occasion of a letter from Bishop Campbell to Thomas Brett which springs a major surprise. Complaining that he had not been informed of Collier's death, he wrote:

> I take it ill that I was not apprized of it that I might have attended him to his grave as I did his first wife.

There is no other known record of this first marriage nor of the part that first wife played in his life. Henry Broxap in his history of the Non-jurors asserts however, but without quoting a source, that Collier left no descendants.

His writings, however, continued to make their impact after his death. His *Ecclesiastical History* had no rival for at least a hundred years. The Non-jurors' service book was later to influence the compilers of the Scottish Episcopalian liturgy and, much later, to influence the authors of the 1928 *Anglican Prayer Book* and, more indirectly, the 1980 *Alternative Service Book*. Meanwhile, the *Short View* and its sequels changed the course of English drama.

2

The Restoration Theatre

For eighteen years, the Puritans had had it all their own way. Throughout the period of Cromwell's Commonwealth, the theatres had been closed by law on the grounds that public stage plays did not "well agree with the seasons of humiliation". In reality, the 1642 Act of Parliament which demanded the closure of the theatres and forbade the performance of any play was only the climax of a festering war of attrition waged by the increasingly powerful puritan middle-class against the stage. What is more, the passing of the Act not only stifled theatrical activity for nearly two decades, many would say it killed theatre as a popular entertainment for several centuries. There was certainly no place for the equivalent of Shakespeare's groundlings in the Restoration theatre. Perhaps it was only with the music halls of the nineteenth century that it regained a wider appeal. Others would say it remains an élitist entertainment late into the twentieth century.

Private Theatre

Despite the 1642 ordinance, there were, however, some secret and private performances and plays were published even though they could not be legally performed. One man in particular provided a link between the pre-Commonwealth theatre and that of the Restoration.

Sir William Davenant (1606-68) was a royalist said to be involved in various plots to restore the monarchy and, for a time, was part of the King's Court in exile on the continent. Back in England in the early 1650s, he was imprisoned but somehow gained Cromwell's pardon. By 1656, he was organising dramatic entertainments in private places. In 1658 he produced two of his own plays, *The Cruelty of the Spaniards in Peru* and *The History of Sir Francis Drake*. It has to be said that they lack dramatic merit but they are evidence that some sort of drama existed during the Commonwealth.

Then, in April 1660, King Charles II was recalled from the continent where, among other things, he had gained a taste for the theatre. But it was a taste for something rather different from the English tradition. Nor was he alone. Many of the English gentry, during the Court's exile in Paris and Brussels, had become familiar with the French theatre of Molière and others which was not only tolerated but respected. Consequently, when the London theatres reopened after the Restoration, the re-established English Court, together with London society, demanded the wit, polish and spectacle of the classical drama of the Grand Siècle. The dramatists responded. In the forty years from 1660-1700, they created a remarkable body of literature. Over 400 new plays, or substantial revisions, were written and produced.

The Playhouses

This new theatre was novel in practical ways. Gone were the open air playhouses of Shakespeare's time, derived from the inn yards visited by touring players. The model for the Restoration theatre was Parisian, with its seated spectators in an indoor space. There were to be other innovations as the century progressed: increasingly elaborate scenery and impressive costumes. Most famously, female characters were now to be played by women rather than by boys as had been the case in Shakespeare's theatre - a development noted by Samuel Pepys in his diary as early as 3 January 1661:

> To the theatre, where was acted *Beggar's Bush*, it being very well done; and here the first time that I ever saw a woman come upon the stage.

Just as the Elizabethans had thought it scandalous that a woman should appear on stage, so Charles claimed to be morally outraged by

14

the idea of boys dressing up as women. He also liked the realism, believing that with this innovation plays would be "esteemed not only harmless delights but useful and instructive representations of human life". However, he seems not to have been offended by the sight of women dressing up as men: so-called "breeches rôles" were popular throughout the Restoration period - the breeches in question being usually tight-fitting! Actresses and actors became seventeenth century celebrities. They were no longer technically outlaws as they had been at the beginning of the century.

Another major change was in the management of the theatres. Back in May 1660 as news spread about King Charles's enjoyment of theatrical entertainments, several groups of enterprising actors had formed themselves into companies. Charles, however, decided to permit just two patent companies under royal patronage - despite the fact that Elizabethan London, with a smaller population than Restoration London's, had supported at least six companies of actors at a time. The two new companies of actors were to be known as *The King's Men* and *The Duke's Men* and the men chosen by the King to run these two companies were, respectively, Thomas Killigrew and, now legally in charge of a theatre, Sir William Davenant. Both had shared, at least in part, the King's exile; both had written plays, in Killigrew's case before the Civil Wars. Both knew the King and his courtiers (they had shared adversity and more agreeable adventures) and exactly what entertainments pleased the Court. Consequently, they were given grants by the King to carry out this work: early examples of subsidised theatre.

There was some rivalry between the two. Killigrew managed to open his theatre, the King's House, in November 1660; Davenant followed in June 1661 with the Duke's House. He, however, was able to use the first rudimentary stage scenery. Because of the rivalry and haste, both had opted to convert existing buildings: namely, indoor tennis courts. Killigrew moved to new and better premises, a former riding school, in 1663 where he too could use scenery. Davenant countered by employing an architect to design a purpose-built theatre - his chosen architect being Sir Christopher Wren. The new Duke's Theatre opened in 1671 in Dorset Garden, near the Thames and just south of Fleet Street. The following year, the King's House famously burned down. Killigrew now also employed Wren to design him a theatre and the new King's House, the Theatre Royal, opened in 1674 in Bridges Street. It was the ancestor of all subsequent Drury Lane theatre buildings.

Unlike the Shakespearean theatre, which welcomed audiences from all classes, these new theatres were at first upper-class venues. In the prologue to his 1672 play, *Marriage à la Mode*, John Dryden described the three main components of the Restoration audience as being "the Town, the City and the Court". Up until that time, however, the dominant group seems to have been the courtiers, together with their hangers-on from the world of fashion, centred on what was London's developing West End. It should be noted that, at this time, the Court was a youthful and lively set. But the prominence of courtiers in the audience did not mean others were not present. Pepys notes that his colleagues in the Navy Office attended. So too, presumably, did officials from other government departments. The Royals themselves regularly visited the public playhouses or saw plays performed at Court.

A by-product of the theatre's limited clientele was the impossibility of a long run for even the most successful play. That said, audiences were prepared to watch a play more than once. On 22 May 1668, the assiduous playgoer Pepys noted:

> Thence to the Duke of York's House to a play, and saw *Sir Martin Marr-all* [by Dryden], where the house is full; and though I have seen it, I think, ten times, yet the pleasure I have is yet as great as ever, and is undoubtedly the best comedy ever was wrote.

Perhaps because of their regular attendances, this principally upper-class audience came to regard the theatres very much as *their* social meeting places, with the actual play no more than a part of the afternoon's entertainment. Pepys recorded the practicalities of getting a seat:

> At a little past twelve to get a good place in the pit [performances usually began at 3.00-3.30pm] against the new play and there setting a poor man to keep my place, I out, and spent an hour at Martin's, my bookseller's, and so back again, where I find the house quite full. But I had my place.

The capacity of the theatres is a matter for conjecture. We do know that attendances at Drury Lane on two December nights in 1677 were

251 and 514 - not large for a city with a population of half a million and confirmation that theatre-going was not a widespread activity. Indeed, attendances fell until the point was reached in 1682 when the two companies, The King's Men and The Duke's, combined and acted as a single company in the Theatre Royal, Drury Lane.

But even in the earlier years of the period in question, you did not go to the theatre just to see a play. Long intervals between the traditional five acts provided time for showing off your clothes and jewellery, for being seen and making assignations - activities quite as important as actually watching, or even listening to, the play. Samuel Pepys has left us a record of how he once, fairly happily, failed to hear a complete performance:

> To the King's House to *The Maid's Tragedy*: but vexed all the while with two talking ladies and Sir Charles Sedley [something of a rake], yet pleased to hear their discourse, he being a stranger. And one of the ladies would and did sit with her mask on, all the play and, being exceedingly witty as ever I heard woman, did talk most pleasantly with him; but was, I believe, a virtuous woman and of quality. He would fain know who she was, but she would not tell; yet did give him many pleasant hints of her knowledge of him, by that means setting his brains at work to find out who she was, and did give him leave to use all means to find out who she was but pulling off her mask. He was mightily witty and she also, making sport of him very inoffensively, that a more pleasant rêncontre I never heard. By that means lost the pleasure of the play wholly.

There were other distractions. Wits among the audience would interrupt the performance, bantering with the actors. The orange-sellers would stand with their backs to the stage noisily advertising their wares - sold primarily to defeat other smells in the crowded auditorium rather than as refreshment. A visiting Frenchman, Henri Misson in his *Memoirs and Observations in his Travels over England* (1698), has left us a clear picture of the later Restoration theatre:

> The pit is an amphitheatre filled with benches without backboards, and covered with green cloth. Men of quality, particularly the younger sort, some ladies of reputation and virtue, and an abundance of damsels that hunt for prey, sit altogether in this place, higgledy-piggledy, chatter, toy, play, hear, hear not. Farther up, against the wall, under the first gallery, and just opposite to the stage, rises another amphitheatre which is taken

17

up by persons of the best quality, among whom are generally very few men.

The historian, James Wright, describes the extent of prostitution in the London theatres at the same time (a "vizard" being either a mask worn as a disguise, or a mask-wearing prostitute):

The playhouses are so extremely pestered with vizard masks and their trade, (occasioning continual quarrels and abuses) that many of the more civilised part of the town are uneasy in the company and shun the theatre as they would a house of scandal.

Gentlemen among the audience would also find their way backstage and to the actresses' dressing-rooms, as Pepys did on more than one occasion, in the company of the actress Mrs Elizabeth Knepp:

To the Duke of York's playhouse, but the house so full, it being a new play *The Coffee House* [Sir Thomas St Serfe], that we could not get in, and so to the King's House. And there, going in, met with Knepp and she took us up into the tiring rooms and to the women's shift where Nell was dressing herself and was all unready and is very pretty, prettier than I thought. And so walked all up and down the house above and then below into the scene room and there sat down and she gave us fruit; and here I read the questions to Knepp while she answered me through her part of *Flora's Figary* [*Flora's Vagaries* by Richard Rhodes] which was acted today. But Lord! To see how they were both painted would make a man mad and did make me loath them; and what base company of men comes among them.

The fact that women were now allowed to act in public encouraged dramatists to write passionate love scenes and to include much bawdy and provocative language. As has been pointed out, women would, at some performances, take the part of the young rake, as happened at times with Vanbrugh's *The Relapse*. Young children, usually girls, were employed to speak bawdy epilogues.

It is important to view this embrace by the theatre of what some would call debauchery and others freedom in a wider historical and social context. As J. W. Krutch points out in his *Comedy and Conscience after the Restoration*:

The Puritans had tended to regard all pleasure as sinful, and they [the courtiers] determined to regard no pleasure as such. The Puritans had condemned the May-pole and ordered that Christmas should be kept as a day of fast; so the courtiers of Charles determined to carry pleasure and gallantry even to divine service, and Charles himself ordered that church music should be such as he could beat time to. Instead of whipping actors at the cart tail, they received the women as mistresses; and instead of forbidding all plays however innocent, they encouraged all however indecent.

There were also those, and especially those who had been associated with Cromwell's régime, who now found it diplomatic to throw off the moral shackles. Being debauched was a very easy way to prove you had not been a Puritan. As Dryden has one of his characters say in *The Wild Gallant* (1663):

He has been a great fanatic formerly, and now has got a habit of swearing that he may be thought a cavalier."

This cult of libertinism was indeed reactionary; an overthrowing by young men of the pruderies and oppression of Puritanism. But there was also a strange blend of refinement, sensuality and, contradictorily, aggression about it. This blend was due in part to the new fashion for things classical - as exemplified by the French playwrights. But grafted onto this interest was an appreciation, also discovered during exile, of the ruthlessness taught by the Italian Machiavelli, together with the teachings of the English philosopher, Thomas Hobbes.

So far as Restoration England was concerned, the influence of Hobbes was crucial. His status as a Court favourite must have meant that his work was required reading for all pretenders to wit. In his *Leviathan* (1651), he concludes that the human being is little more than a competitive animal, concerned only with the pursuit of power and the gratification of bodily appetites. What made him so popular in the Stuart Court was that he went on to claim that an absolute monarchy was the only defence against human violence. What made him so attractive to the young libertines and rakes of the Court's outer circles was the fact that his arguments could be used to defend both sensuality and ruthlessness. After all, had not the great philosopher implied, wasn't it only natural to satisfy one's appetites, to reject the constraints of a moral or puritanical authority? And had not Hobbes also said that it was equally natural to behave aggressively in order to win satisfaction? Hence, as tender modern souls see it, the savagery of much Restoration comedy.

The Plays

'Restoration Drama' is obviously a wider term than 'Restoration Comedy'; and while the concern of this book is the latter because, largely, it was Collier's preoccupation, it should not be forgotten that the new enthusiasm for the theatre generated by King Charles's accession in 1660 embraced a much greater variety of drama than the dozen or so Restoration comedies that are still regularly revived.

In the years immediately following the Restoration, there appeared a number of political plays, many of them satirising or frankly jeering at the defeated Puritans. There were musical dramas and romances as well as heroic dramas, often tragedies, in which 'supermen' grappled with doomed love and questions of honour in exotic, classical settings. The latter owed more than a little to the French tragedian Corneille (1606-84) and appealed to the dashing young courtiers and adventurers who formed a significant part of the audience.

Despite the expectations of the audience, the authors of some of these plays could, in their early attempts to adopt French theatrical conventions, be bombastic and dull. Aristotle's dramatic unities were followed - sometimes slavishly. Pale imitations of the French twelve-syllable Alexandrine line dragged their "weary length along". Yet the main failing of the immediate post-Restoration drama was not the absence of humour, weak structure or dull language, but the lack of grace - typified by near-farcical comedies such as Dryden's *Mr Limberham*.

There was also some romantic or sentimental drama, foreshadowing the comedy of the eighteenth century; as, for example, Dryden's *The Rival Ladies* (1664). But soon there developed what is commonly accepted as Restoration Comedy, the elegant comedy of manners and intrigue. The material for this new form was the life and loves of the ladies and gentlemen of the Court together with the fops and other hangers-on. Their manners, morals and social customs were put on display. Sex and money, and how to get them, were the basis of the plots. Written with verve, oozing energy, the plays celebrated pleasure and ambition without reserve. Too often, twentieth century revivals have over-emphasised the elegance of the characters and have laboured the epigrams and aphorisms. There was little that was languid about most Restoration comedies. And both dramatists and audiences of the day would have been bemused by one or two revivals in the 1990s which have attempted to play up the cruelty of the plots and intrigues at the expense of their comedy.

This 'comedy of manners' may have evolved in response to new habits and new values, but it also had points of contact with the earlier 'comedy of character' of Ben Jonson and his contemporaries. Both traditions satirised human failings, and both eschewed romance and sentiment. Both, incidentally, gave their characters descriptive sur-names. But there are differences. Jonson regularly pictured the lower strata of society. The characters of the Restoration comedies may be no more decent than Jonson's but they are from the top drawer of their times. While Jonson was mocking any lapse from wise living, the Restoration dramatists were pre-occupied with laughing at failures to live up to the current fashions of high society.

At the risk of over-simplification, it is possible to list certain qualities that those fashions demanded of the ideal society gentleman: he must be well born; he must dress well, but not ostentatiously; he must be poised and witty; he must be a skilled love-maker - preferably with several ladies; his head must be master of his heart; he must be discreet; he must conceal any serious passion; he must not show love or jealousy towards his wife. Any deviation from this code of behaviour was material for the comic writer or satirist.

Those who did not even profess to follow the trends of fashion were also liable to attack by the dramatists. Clergymen, squires, merchants and men of letters were always greeted with laughter when one was introduced into a group of Court wits and their ladies. But those who professed to follow the code yet failed in their attempts attracted the most derisive mockery. The too-careful fop, the laborious wit, the boastful coquette were all considered prime subjects for ridicule. The character who fell in love and allowed true emotion to show was also intrinsically comic, indeed a farcical character. Consequently marriage was one of the seventeenth century stock jokes.

It is possible to go further in describing a 'typical' Restoration comedy. To quote J. W. Krutch again:

The scene is usually London, and the chief persons, with few exceptions, members of high society. If the country or any city besides London is introduced, it is only for the purpose of ridicule. 'The country is as terrible, I find, to our English ladies, as a monastery to those abroad; and on my virginity, I think they would rather marry a London gaoler, than a high sheriff of a county, since neither can stir from his employment', says one of the characters in *The Country Wife*, and the attitude is typical. The scene moves usually in a restricted circle: the drawing room, the park, the bed chamber, the tavern, then the drawing room again, through which scenes move a set of ever recurring types - the graceful young rake, the faithless wife, the deceived husband, and, perhaps, a charming young heroine who is to be bestowed in the end on the rake.

He notes other recurring elements of Restoration drama:

Another type of character . . . is the so-called 'false ingénue', whose characteristic is ignorance but not innocence. Mrs Pinchwife in *The Country Wife* and Miss Prue in *Love for Love* are good examples. Vanbrugh has two, Hoyden in *The Relapse* and Corinna in *The Confederacy*.

Krutch also makes this significant observation:

If the pursuit of women was the principal business of life for the characters of these comedies, marriage was the most dreaded calamity ... and though many comedies end with the marriage, no happy married couples figure on the stage.

The dramatist George Farquhar summarised the necessities of a good comedy more succinctly:

A play without a beau, cully [a fool or dupe], cuckold, or coquette, is as poor an entertainment to some palates, as their Sunday's dinner would be without beef and pudding.

Society, after eighteen years' of state Puritanism, was busy living to the top of its bent - which frequently meant sexual excess and experimentation and always sensual gratification. Not surprisingly, an age without ethical objections to libertinism produced a drama without moral overtones. The acquiescent cuckold was a figure of scorn, yet jealousy of a wife's lover was bad taste. As Professor Dobrée writes in his *Restoration Drama*:

How could it [Restoration comedy] avoid dealing with sex when its distinguishing feature down to Congreve is that it is concerned with the attempt to rationalise sexual relationships? . . . Sex in Congreve is a battle of the wits. It is not a battlefield of the emotions.

The playwrights, in order to gain a living, had to write to please the Court. Professor Dobrée maintains that Restoration comedy expressed "not licentiousness, but a deep curiosity, and a desire to try new ways of living".

In his *A History of Restoration Drama*, Allardyce Nicholl suggests that because the dramatists mirrored their age, they cannot be criticised. As Shakespeare and Jonson had done, so did they. They held a mirror up to life, and wrote down what they saw. The Court, rather than the theatre, needed censure, for the drama was the exclusive entertainment of the leisured class. And as J. W. Krutch also observed:

> The Restoration stage was a fashionable entertainment where the most reckless of the upper class saw their follies and vices wittily and realistically presented.

The dramatists were indeed holding a mirror up to nature.

However, this is not only a defence but a criticism of Restoration comedy and manners as P. A. W. Collins pointed out in a somewhat censorious essay in the 1957 *Pelican Guide to English Literature*, Vol. IV:

> The preoccupation with love (in both tragedy and comedy), the stress on sex-antagonism, the common conventions that marriage is a bore and love primarily or exclusively a physical appetite - all these are ... typically immature attitudes.

Despite the apparent licence relished by the dramatists, they never had complete freedom. The roots of a distinctly muddled situation had been laid in pre-Commonwealth times. A Court official, the Master of the Revels, had been responsible for licensing and censoring all plays. He in turn was responsible to the Lord Chamberlain - and actually *paid* £150 per year to perform the duty. In the summer following the Restoration, Charles II confirmed Sir Henry Herbert, who had held the appointment before the time of Cromwell, in the post. Not only was he entitled to charge £1 per play, new or old, for it to be licensed for a new performance, but he also claimed the right to licence billiards, fencing, organists, dancing masters, the proprietor of a waxworks and a showman who exhibited two dromedaries. In all, he amassed some £4,000 a year - hence his readiness to pay to do the job!

But before re-appointing Herbert, Charles had also just granted patents or authorities to Killigrew and Davenant giving them exclusive rights to run the only two theatres. He also decreed that Killigrew and Davenant "do not at any time hereafter cause to be acted or represented any play, interlude, or opera, containing any manner of profanation, scurrility or obscenity" - so making them their own censors. Spotting a considerable restriction on his income, Herbert petitioned the King. He sued Davenant and several actors but to no real avail. Then in 1673 he died. Killigrew took over as Master of Revels, thus becoming both manager and censor. When he died, his son Charles Killigrew grabbed the post and stayed in power for forty years.

All the various holders of this office seem to have regarded the post as simply a lucrative sinecure, entitling them to receive fees merely in return for a nod of approval. There is also evidence to show that plays were often performed without a licence. Just occasionally the Lord Chamberlain himself intervened, but almost always to censor historical plays on the political ground that parallels could be drawn with contemporary events. Once he stopped a revival of Beaumont and Fletcher's 1619 play *The Maid's Tragedy*, presumably because it depicted events not unlike ones towards the end of Charles I's reign. In 1680 he stopped a play for its "scandalous expressions and reflections upon the Government". Even adaptations of Shakespeare's *Richard II* and *Henry VI* were forbidden because parallels might be drawn with the present King. Occasionally a play was censored on religious grounds. For example, Shadwell's *The Lancashire Witches* was severely cut in 1681 for supposedly ridiculing both Anglican and Roman Catholic priests.

During the reigns of Charles II and James II, however, no-one thought to censor plays for their sexual content or even language. Sexual licence was the fashion. In this connection, it is interesting to note the constantly changing fashions in profanities, as does Geoffrey Hughes in his book *Swearing*. Until the decline of religious faith in the twentieth centuries, blasphemies and profanities, such as "Christ", "Jesus" and even "God", were the most taboo words. These were then replaced by the largely four-letter, sexual words. The most modern social surveys imply that these have in turn been replaced by words deemed politically incorrect, so that "bitch", "cripple" and "slag" can cause greater offence than, say, "fuck".

There were some attempts at self-regulation by the theatres - though mainly of the audiences. On 2 February 1673, this poster was displayed at the entrances to the playhouses:

Whereas complaint has often been made to us that diverse persons do rudely press and with evil language and blows force their way into our theatres [the Theatre Royal in Bridges Street and the Duke's Theatre in Dorset Garden] at the time of their public representations and acting, without paying the price established at both the said theatres, to the great disturbance of our servants, licensed by our authority, as well as others, and to the danger of the public peace; our will and pleasure therefore is, and we do hereby straightly charge and command, that no person of what quality soever do presume to come into either of the said theatres before and during the time of acting and until the plays are quite finished, without paying the price established for the respective places . . . And, our will and command is that no person of what quality soever presume to stand or sit on the stage, or to come within any part of the scenes, before the play begins, while 'tis acting, or after 'tis ended.

The audiences remained rowdy. In 1680, "some gentlemen in their cups" interrupted a performance by "speaking ill" of one of the actors and, more importantly, of one of the King's mistresses. The theatre was closed "till His Majesty's further pleasure" and the heckler prosecuted for riotous behaviour.

But the nature of the 'new' drama was also under attack from its beginnings. The diarist John Evelyn, "a man of means, of unblemished character" to quote *The Oxford Companion to English Literature* and a man respected both at Court and in the town, had deplored the license of the stage soon after the Restoration. In February 1664 (1665 in the new style calendar), he wrote in a letter to Viscount Cornberry, in which he also carefully stressed that he was "far from Puritanism":

It [acting] is not allowed in any city of Christendom so much as in this one town of London, where there are more wretched and obscene plays permitted than in all the world beside . . . Plays are now with us become a licentious excess and a vice and need severe censors that should as well to their morality, as to their lines and numbers.

Sir Richard Blackmore, a minor poet and later physician to Queen Anne, complained in his preface to *Prince Arthur* that the poets used "all their wit in opposition to religion, and to the destruction of virtue and good manners in the world". With an intensity typical of the later

Augustans, he roundly declared: "The poet must instruct." Comedy should laugh men out of their vices, as tragedy should frighten men. In his earnestness, he is perhaps Collier's nearest predecessor. In 1689, one Robert Gould wrote a vicious and poetic satire entitled *The Playhouse*. In it he claimed:

> In short, our plays are now so loosely writ,
> They've neither manners, modesty or wit.
> How can these things to our instruction had
> Which are unchaste to see, a crime to read?

He was later unable to get any publisher to accept his work.

But such critics were not isolated voices. Indeed, it must not be forgotten that, in the forty years following the Restoration, "many a Puritan still lived" to quote J. W. Krutch. Certainly, to judge by the number of religious tracts and broadsides published in the Restoration years, the great majority of readers were pious, prudent and possessed of what can anachronistically be called a middle-class morality. Most were probably unconcerned about, or at least unaware of, theatrical fashions. What had changed, as I pointed out earlier, was that the expanding town or city contained a new and increasingly vociferous merchant class, who were increasingly aware of what went on at Court and in the theatres. Indeed, there soon developed a real antagonism between the 'respectable' traders and merchants of the city and a pleasure-seeking Court. To the solid, sober, industrious merchant, the wealthy rakes of West End society personified laziness and lechery. They had nothing to do all day but pleasure themselves. On the other hand, 'West Enders' saw the City men as petty, jealous and sexually inadequate. The antagonism was resolved only after the accession of the relatively strait-laced William III. Yet, though he was apparently shocked by what he heard of what went on in the theatre, his wife, Mary, occasionally attended public performances until her death from smallpox in 1694.

Despite this moral shift at Court, the plays of the last decade of the century followed the fashions earlier set by Wycherley and Etherege. Indeed, writing in the late eighties and nineties, the playwright Thomas D'Urfey and his fellow hack-writers consciously set out to oppose middle-class morality. Yet, as the stage became more and more dependent on support from the town, reform of the drama began - however slowly at first.

A turning point was reached in 1696 when Colley Cibber's obtrusively moral play *Love's Last Shift* was a success. In it, the rakish hero is reclaimed by his faithful wife. Loveless, the rake, shows a good deal of earthy realism and pungency in his speeches, but Amanda's speeches can fairly be said, to quote P. A. W. Collins, to be "preposterously unconvincing".

Just before the turn of the century, the stage was indeed ready for re-orientation and Jeremy Collier was only part of a general trend of opinion demanding reform of the drama. As we shall see, the question as to precisely how important a part of the trend he was is a matter for debate.

Some have seen him as a single-handed giant purging the country of its ills. As Allardyce Nicholl pointed out in his *A History of Restoration Drama*, it was at one time believed that Collier was almost wholly responsible "for a violent revulsion of feeling with regard to contemporary comedy." Others see him as an ineffectual Cassandra. But his pungent, rather than trenchant, *Short View* was successful partly because it stated what a number of people had been thinking over the past few decades. More importantly, it enjoyed all the success that publicity could bring it. In 1698, Collier was already a notorious figure. Still an outlaw, he had no legal right to be in London. Yet in the *Short View* he boldly attacked those who had been the favoured writers of Charles II and James II. He was also an outcast from his church, and yet he still considered himself a priest, and practised as one. He was not just a middle-class moralist. He was a controversial figure of his time who suddenly turned his attention to the stage and fanned a smouldering discussion into a great blaze of reforming enthusiasm.

His motivation is a matter of speculation. Was it moral certitude, first nurtured at Knole? Was it simply an awareness of what was being talked about in the City? Or had he seen Vanbrugh's play *The Provoked Wife* (1697) in which a character exclaims:

Kind Heaven! Inspire some venom'd priest to write?"
If it were the latter, heaven did.

3

The *Short View*

In the opening sentence of the introduction to his *Short View*, Collier provides his definition of the purpose of drama:

The business of plays is to recommend virtue and discountenance vice; to show the uncertainty of humane greatness, the sudden turns of fate, and the unhappy conclusions of violence and injustice.

Throughout the rest of his "short", verbose would be as accurate, argument, he never admits it might have any other purpose - such as, for example, entertainment. The *Short View* is a rumbustious, helter-skelter analysis of the ways in which Restoration drama, and comedy in particular, failed to match his vision of what the stage might be. He is "as sure of himself as only a hopeless fanatic can be", to quote J. W. Krutch's *Comedy and Conscience After the Restoration* and he possessed "an unholy joy in combat, where he lays about him with all the exultation of Samson slaying Philistines".

Collier was a fighter. Not a satirist; not an academic critic, calmly developing a considered case. His stated ambition and his purpose was reform. His real aim was, perhaps, the complete closure of the theatre.

As we have said, his motivation can only be a matter for speculation. It is indeed probable that he developed a distaste for matters theatrical at Knole. Some critics have suggested that his

28

opinions may have been formed simply from his reading of play texts or possibly by visiting the theatre - presumably strictly on business. Thomas Brown in his satirical play *The Stage Beaux Toss'd in a Blanket* certainly hints that Collier did attend and hypocritically enjoyed what he saw. That Collier wrote "Lovelace" instead of Loveless and "Lord Foplington" instead of Lord Foppington in *The Relapse* suggests mis-hearing rather than mis-reading. What cannot be disputed is the fact that profanity and morality were talking points among the chattering classes of 1698. Narcissus Luttrell (1657-1732), the compiler of a chronicle of contemporary events, informs us that much concern had been expressed by King and Parliament about these matters and that, in consequence, measures had been proposed for their suppression. For Thursday, February 10, 1697 (1698 new style) Luttrell makes this entry:

The Commons . . . ordered an address to his majesty to suppress prophaneness and immorality.

Between this date and March 5 three other entries of a similar nature are to be found in Luttrell's work. On March 5, the following item appears:

The Justices of Peace of Middlesex have made an order that the constables go to all public houses, to caution them to observe His Majesty's proclamation against prophaneness.

There is, incidentally, some debate as to the precise publication date of the *Short View*. The Preface is dated "Mar. 5, 1697/8" - that is, 1697 by the old calendar, 1698 by the new style. However, one critic, D. Crane Taylor, writing on William Congreve in 1931 asserts:

Collier's *Short View* was published on Thursday, April 21, 1698, six weeks later than has hitherto been supposed. The announcement of the first edition appears only in the *Flying Post* for Tuesday, April 19, to Thursday, April 21, 1698 . . . Critics have invariably assigned the first issue of the *Short View* to March because the preface to the first edition was dated March 5, 1698.

Another certain and important influence on Collier was the critic Thomas Rymer (1641-1713), whose style and methods he closely followed. Rymer began his career by translating from the French a critical work on Aristotle by René Rapin. Then, in 1677, he began to write on his own account about English tragic drama. He denounced playwrights for technical matters such as implausibilities in plot and characterisation but repeatedly returned to one particular obsession - that drama should concern itself with ideals. This principle led him to maintain that poetic justice must prevail in every play: that is, the virtuous must triumph while the wicked must be damned or at least punished. This view, as we shall see, underpins much of Collier's writing and that of his disciples.

Rymer's conviction that plays should portray an ordered and orderly universe also led him to insist on what he termed "decorum". By this he meant that characters should be fair or "typical" representatives of their social rank and occupation. This was a concept he had adopted from Rapin who had stated that the poet, and therefore playwright, should:

> . . . exhibit every person in his proper character: a slave with base thoughts and servile inclinations; a prince with liberal heart and air of majesty; a soldier, fierce, insolent, surly, inconstant; an old man, covetous, wary, jealous."

From this, Rymer went on to rule that the distinguishing characteristic of any woman is modesty - not a view shared by the typical Restoration dramatist. Despite this, Rymer's views were widely respected. In his published writings, if not in private, Dryden deferred to Rymer on more than one occasion. In 1681, Nahum Tate produced his infamous adaptation of *King Lear* - complete with a happy ending based on the triumph of poetic justice for all concerned!

In 1692, Rymer himself turned his attention to Shakespeare's plays in his *Short View of Tragedy*. A fair snapshot of his view of that playwright can be found in his assessment of one of the great tragedies: "There is not . . . a pig in Barbary that has not a truer taste of things than Othello." This was the critic that Collier admired most; the only literary critic to whom he acknowledged any debt.

Indeed, besides borrowing his title from Rymer, Collier applauds himself for applying to Restoration comedy the good sense with which Rymer attacked Shakespeare. In Collier's eyes, Rymer was perfectly correct in damning Shakespeare for being "too guilty to make an evidence." His reason? - "When there is most smut there is least sense."

Given this depth of analysis, it will be apparent that the *Short View* is not well argued. His later pamphlets were more succinct and more convincing. The *Short View* is, however, undoubtedly the most famous of his publications - as well as being the one which stimulated the controversy. Therefore, at this point, it is worth summarising its argument - which, in fact, has been admirably done in one sentence by J. W. Krutch:

> [Collier] gathered together all the weapons, religious, moral and ascetic, that could be turned against the stage, and flung himself upon it with a fury and an exultation that seems to have left the wits momentarily stunned.

In more detail, Collier's introductory argument is this. First, poetry is noble and its purpose is "to recommend virtue." The poets therefore have a strong and noble weapon with which to fight vice. But, at this time, 1698, the craft of poetry and, by extension, drama has fallen into bad hands. Additionally, the moral state of society is deplorable. Nothing has served to bring about this debauchery as much as has the playhouse - thanks to the contemporary dramatists. Far from fighting vice they are indifferent to morality.

The next step in his argument follows his own debatable logic. Because they are indifferent to morality, they must be therefore virtue's declared enemies. His triumphant and martyr-like conclusion is that, in order to attack virtue most effectually, the dramatists have "craftily" attacked the chief advocates of virtue: namely, the priests and the Church. To quote again from his introduction:

> That this complaint is not unreasonable I shall endeavour to prove by showing the misbehaviour of the stage with respect to morality and religion. Their liberties in the following particulars are intolerable, viz. their smuttiness of expression; their swearing, profaneness, and lewd application of scripture; their abuse of the clergy; their making their top characters libertines, and giving them success in their debauchery.

His various charges are grouped in chapters though, in the last part of the book, he returns to many of his earlier themes - only with more venom and more evidence.

Thus his first chapter deals with the *Immodesty of the Stage*. Unlike the literary critic who illustrates his or her arguments with quotation from the text under discussion, Collier states that he does not intend to set down chapter and page nor to cite long passages:

Indeed the passages, many of them, are in no condition to be handled. He that is desirous to see these flowers - let him do it in their own soil. 'Tis my business rather to kill the root than transplant it.

Nevertheless, he does quote some examples, though not always those that might most effectively prove his case.

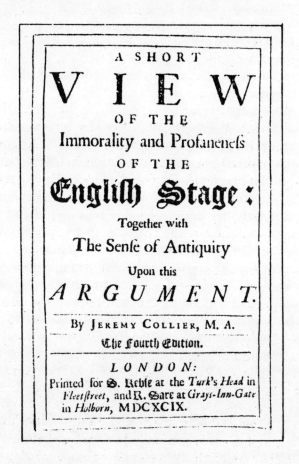

A SHORT

VIEW

OF THE

Immorality and Profaneneſs

OF THE

𝕰𝖓𝖌𝖑𝖎𝖘𝖍 𝕾𝖙𝖆𝖌𝖊 :

Together with

The Senſe of Antiquity

Upon this

A R G U M E N T.

By JEREMY COLLIER, M. A.

The Fourth Edition.

LONDON:

Printed for S. Keble at the *Turk's Head* in *Fleetſtreet*, and R. Sare at *Grays-Inn-Gate* in *Holborn*, MDCXCIX.

Figure 2: *A Short View*

One of his recurring arguments in this first chapter is that lewdness of language raises evil passions, is unworthy of a gentleman and degrades man to the level of beasts - "Goats and monkeys, if they could speak, would express their brutality in such language as this." Wycherley's *The Country Wife* and *The Plain Dealer* are attacked severely for what Collier calls immodesty and lewdness, and for their debauchery which appears in the plays in both "image and description; sometimes by way of allusion; sometimes in disguise; and sometimes without it". He believes the passions aroused by such lewdness as exists in these and similar plays can only be "satisfied with a crime" - the same argument which today claims that screen pornography and violence encourage imitation. Although Wycherley is called by Collier, on another occasion, "a man of good sense", he is here wholeheartedly damned for his "masterly Hand" in the presentation of lewdness.

Collier follows this with a particular complaint: that "the poets [dramatists] make women speak smuttily." By "women" he means ladies of quality. He goes on to object to any adulation or approval of immodesty in such female characters. Here he does actually give an example from Congreve's *The Double Dealer*: "There are but four ladies in this play, and three of the biggest of them are whores." He compares this with the classical plays of Terence and Plautus whom the class-conscious Collier excuses on the grounds that their "strumpets were little people".

He has other specific complaints. He objects to any emphasised double meanings - "the worst is generally turned to the audience" - and to prologues and epilogues in which the authors advocate vice in their own voices and not from within "the cloak of one of their characters". But what offends him most of all is any association between smut and religion. He is particularly scandalised by Vanbrugh who, in *The Relapse*, has Lord Foppington remark,

> Sunday is a vile day, I must confess. A man must have very little to do at church that can give an account of the sermon.

Collier accepts this as the dramatist's opinion, never acknowledging that Foppington - an unemployed wastrel, an extreme fop and a social butterfly - might have been created as an object of ridicule.

For Collier, satire is neither defence nor excuse. For him, such characters must be concealed rather than exhibited for ridicule upon the stage. In fairness to him, it must be admitted that, while Foppington was definitely an object of ridicule in the eyes of the courtly audiences on account of his excesses and failures to follow fashion, fops of the Court, only a little less exotic than Foppington, were admired and copied.

We learn here that Collier knew what went on in the playhouses. He is incensed that any of the stage lewdness is tolerated by ladies of quality in the audience:

Do the women leave all the regards to decency and conscience behind them, when they come to the playhouse? . . . Were their pretences to sobriety elsewhere nothing but hypocrisy and grimace?

The remainder of this first chapter of the *Short View* is devoted to a long series of examples taken from the works of Plautus, Terence, Seneca, Æschylus, Sophocles, Euripides, Ben Jonson, Beaumont, Fletcher and Corneille who, in Collier's eyes, never sin in any of these respects. They depict women of quality, he reports approvingly, with respect and decorum. Rough language is always placed in the mouth of a peasant. Acts and expressions of love are described rarely and then only indirectly. Virtue is seen to triumph; poetic justice prevails. These classical dramatists are the models he would therefore have his contemporaries examine and copy. Aristophanes, incidentally, is not included in his blanket approval of classical drama. Collier judges him to have "had sense, but he does not always use it" and sees one supreme, if anachronistic, reason to dismiss the great comic writer: "His own plays are sufficient to ruin his authority - for he discovers himself a downright atheist." Returning to his own times, Collier concludes:

The present English stage is superlatively scandalous. It exceeds the liberties of all times and countries. It has not so much the poor plea of a precedent . . . A new world of vice found out, and planted with all the industry imaginable.

The second chapter of the *Short View* is concerned with the profanity on stage. Here Collier mounts separate attacks on, firstly, cursing and swearing; and secondly on the abuse of religion and scripture. He passes quickly over the subject of cursing:

What is more frequent then their wishes of hell and confusion, devils
and diseases, all the plagues of this world, and the next, to each other?
On the subject of swearing, he is more loquacious, objecting to the
fact that all manner of characters, gentlemen included, indulge:
"'Tis used by all persons, and upon all occasions: by heroes and
patrons; by gentlemen and clowns." He admits that in this area
"Shakespeare is comparatively sober", but censures the writers of
*The Old Bachelor, The Double Dealer, Love for Love, Don Quixote, The
Provoked Wife* and *The Relapse*. He again objects to "swearing before
women" who "make up a considerable part of the audience".

He spends many pages quoting instances in which characters
speak lightly of "going to heaven or hell" or where they casually
dismiss or discount sin. He condemns *The Double Dealer* because
Congreve has Lady Plyant cry out "Jesu". Dryden is criticised for
improper passages in the introduction of *Aureng-Zebe* (1676) and in
other of his plays. What is surprising is that Collier holds up as his
authority not the Christian scriptures but what he terms "the comparative regularity of the heathen stage". Plautus, Terence and the
Greek tragedians furnish examples of correctness. And rather than
quoting St Paul or the Ten Commandments as reason for not taking
the name of God in vain, Collier cites Thomas Rymer's *Short View
of Tragedy*. It is interesting to conjecture whether Collier felt that, as
he was attacking the stage, he would do better to support his attack
with ammunition from dramatic and literary authorities rather
than theological ones, or whether he simply felt that religion and
the scriptures were best divorced from the playhouses.

He concludes his attack on the profanities employed by the
playwrights with a flurry of rhetorical questions:

Have we not a clearer light to direct us, and greater punishments to
make us afraid? Is there no distinction between truth and fiction,
between majesty and pageant? Must God be treated like an idol . . . ?
Are these the returns we make Him for his supernatural assistance?

Sister Rose Anthony in her account of *The Jeremy Collier Stage
Controversy* makes this fair assessment of his second chapter:

The chapter which Collier devotes to attacking the profaneness of the
stage breathes forth the sincerity of its author; there is no questioning
the fact. Neither can we doubt that the stage-poets, many of them,

were seriously guilty of the charge of profaneness and deserving of every stroke of the reformer's lash. However, one cannot help wishing that Collier had not read into some of the expressions a profanity which the authors never intended; that he had used greater discrimination in selecting his evidence; and that where the poets intended no profaneness, he had written with less impetuosity and less heat."

The third chapter, which is concerned with the abuse of the clergy on stage, shows Collier at his most earnest and humourless. "These poets, I observe, when they grow lazy, and are inclined to nonsense, they commonly get a clergyman to speak it." Somewhat oddly, he again finds his justification in classical works such as those of Homer and Virgil, where priests are presented with proper decorum and respect. He maintains that any satire is an attack not on an individual priest but on the entire sacred profession. He produces an example from Dryden's *The Spanish Friar* where Dominick is called "a parcel of holy guts and garbage", proved to be a knave and ultimately exits in dishonour. Congreve's clerics, such as Saygrace in *The Double Dealer*, are likewise presented as examples of a dramatist's unfair treatment of the clergy. In Collier's view, they are shamefully shown to speak with levity. Saygrace, a family chaplain, is not above entering into an intrigue - and, almost certainly, Collier took this as an affront, if not to himself then to the office which he had once held. Likewise, Vanbrugh is severely reprimanded for his portrayal of Bull, the chaplain in *The Relapse*:

[Bull] wishes the married couple joy, in language horribly smutty and profane. To transcribe it would blot the paper too much.

The speech which so offended Collier is presumably this one:

Bull: I most humbly thank your honours; and I hope, since it has been my lot to join you in the holy bands of wedlock, you will so cultivate the soil, which I have craved a blessing on, that your children may swarm about you like bees about a honeycomb.

Collier is even more horrified that Bull is described as needing "money, preferment, wine and a whore" before he will co-operate with an intrigue: "To expose a priest . . . is an affront to the deity." He goes on to produce examples from the classical writers to illustrate their reverence of the priesthood - notwithstanding it was a priesthood dedicated to the service of what, for Collier, were

pagan gods. He also praises Corneille and Molière for never presenting a priest on stage and points out that there was little ridicule
of the priesthood in the English theatre till the time of Charles II,
dismissing the curate in Shakespeare's *Love's Labour's Lost* on the
grounds that "the whole play is a very silly one". He finally
summarises his argument by insisting on respect for the clergy
because of "their relation to the deity"; "the importance of their
office"; and their historical privilege: the clergy are responsible to
no-one but God. No mere dramatist should therefore presume to
criticise, still less mock, a cleric.

To be fair to Collier, he does admit that not all clerics are faultless
- but he still maintains that is no excuse for censuring the clergy at
large, nor the post or office of priest:

I grant persons and things are not always suited. A good post may be
ill kept, but then the censure should keep close to the fault, and the
office not suffer for the manager. The clergy may have their failings
sometimes like others, but what then? The character is still untarnished.

Chapter Four of the *Short View* is concerned with poetic justice.
Collier argues that because the virtuous often do not triumph or
succeed, the playwrights are encouraging immorality. To quote his
chapter title: "The stage-poets make their principal persons vicious, and reward them at the end of the play." Collier uses
"vicious" with its then general meaning of addicted to vice. He
quotes many characters from various plays who profit by vice:

Wild-blood [in Dryden's *The Mock Astrologer*] sets up for debauchery,
ridicules marriage, and swears by Mahomet. Bellamy makes sport
with the devil, and Lorenzo [in the same playwright's *The Spanish
Friar*] is vicious, and calls his father "bawdy magistrate"; Horner [in
Wycherley's *The Country Wife*] is horridly smutty, and Harcourt false
to his friend who used him kindly. In *The Plain Dealer*, Freeman talks
coarsely, cheats the widow, debauches her son, and makes him un-
dutiful. Bellmour [in Congreve's *The Old Bachelor*] is lewd and profane;
and Mellefont [in Wycherley's *The Double Dealer*] puts Careless in the
best way he can to debauch Lady Plyant.

For once Collier allows himself to quote a text, with sarcasm:

In *The Provoked Wife* [Vanbrugh], Constant swears at length, solicits
Lady Brute, confesses himself lewd, and prefers debauchery to mar-

riage. He handles the last subject very notably and worth the hearing. *"There is* (says he) *a poor sordid slavery in marriage, that turns the flowing tide of honour, and sinks it to the lowest ebb of infamy. 'Tis a corrupted soil: ill nature, avarice, sloth, cowardice, and dirt are all its product. But then constancy* (alias whoring) *is a brave, free, haughty, generous agent."* This is admirable stuff both for the rhetoric and the reason!

He concludes, sarcastically:

To sum up the evidence. A fine gentleman, is a fine whoring, swearing, smutty, atheistical man. These qualifications it seems complete the idea of honour. They are the top-improvements of fortune, and the distinguishing glories of birth and breeding! This is the stage-test for quality, and those that can't stand it ought to be disclaimed. The restraints of conscience and the pedantry of virtue are unbecoming a Cavalier. Future securities and reaching beyond life are vulgar provisions. If he falls a thinking at this rate, he forfeits his honour; for his head was only made to run against a post! Here you have a man of breeding and figure that burlesques the Bible, swears, and talks smut to ladies, speaks ill of his friend behind his back, and betrays his interest. A fine gentleman that has neither honesty nor honour, conscience nor manners, good nature nor civil hypocrisy. Fine only in the insignificancy of life, the abuse of religion, and the scandals of conversation. These worshipful things are the poets' favourites. They appear at the head of the Fashion, and shine in character and equipage.

The female characters are equally as bad an influence, he states:

The fine ladies are of the same cut with the gentlemen. Moraima [in Dryden's *Don Sebastian*] is scandalously rude to her father, helps him to a beating, and runs away with Antonio; Angelica [in Congreve's *Love for Love*] talks saucily to her uncle, and Belinda [in Vanbrugh's *The Provoked Wife*] confesses her inclination for a gallant. And as I have observed already, the topping ladies in *The Mock Astrologer, The Spanish Friar, The Country Wife, The Old Bachelor, Orphan, The Double Dealer* and [Dryden's] *Love Triumphant,* are smutty, and sometime profane.

Collier then digresses to show what admirably moral, young people figure in the works of Plautus and Terence, before reiterating his charge:

What a fine time lewd people have on the English stage. No censure, no mark of infamy, no mortification must touch them. They keep their honour untarnished, and carry off the advantage of their character.

They are set up for the standard of behaviour, and the masters of ceremony and sense. And at last, that the example may work the better, they generally make them rich and happy, and reward them with their own desires.

Dryden's *Preface* to his play *The Mock Astrologer* is then brought forward as evidence that rewarding vice is not only practised but admitted by the playwrights. Indeed, Dryden's self-justifying *Preface* is dismissed by Collier as a "lame defence". When Dryden states he knows of no such law - that virtue must be rewarded and vice punished - Collier replies: "Poets are not always exactly in rule." He will not allow Dryden to quote Plautus, Terence and Ben Jonson in his defence, conveniently forgetting that he has himself used them to make his own case. Collier here magnificently dismisses their evidence on the grounds that "they were poets" and consequently not to be trusted. When Dryden questions "whether instruction has anything to do with comedy", Collier reminds him that Horace praised poets for "reforming manners". Collier reiterates the point in his own distinctive style:

Indeed to make delight the main business of comedy is an unreasonable and dangerous principle: it opens the way to all licentiousness and confounds the distinction between mirth and madness.

Collier is unable to grasp the concept of entertainment.

Having next discussed a number of pre-Restoration plays at some length, Collier then quotes Rymer's hero, the French critic, Monsieur Rapin who affirmed certain principles. First:

That delight is the end that poetry aims at, but not the principal one. For poetry, being an art, ought to be profitable by the quality of its own nature and by the essential subordination that all arts should have to polity [civil order], whose end in general is the public good.

Collier goes on to quote approvingly Ben Jonson when he "lays it down for a principle":

... that 'tis impossible to be a good poet without being a good man. That he (a good poet) is said to be able to inform young men of all good discipline, and enflame grown men to all great virtues.

However, Collier regrets that "nothing but ribaldry, profanation, blasphemy, all licence of offence to God and man is practised." And for Dryden's affirmation that laughter might be a "chief end of comedy", Collier has no time. Such a ridiculous idea "needs no explaining". Three pages later, Collier is still scornful of such a subversive thought:

> Now we know the reason and profaneness and obscenity of the stage, of their hellish cursing and swearing and, in short, of their great industry to make God and goodness contemptible: 'tis all to satisfy the company and make people laugh! A most admirable justification! What can be more engaging to an audience than to see a poet thus aetheistically brave?

He has yet more satirical scorn to pour on Dryden:

> We must make them laugh, right or wrong, for delight is the chief end of comedy. Delight! He should have said debauchery!

By way of a lengthy conclusion to this chapter, Collier turns to the "manners of the stage" or what Rymer would have defined as decorum:

> To succeed in this business, there must always be a regard had to age, sex and condition; and nothing put into the mouths of persons which disagrees with any of these circumstances. 'Tis not enough to say a witty thing, unless it be spoken by a likely person and a proper occasion.

Dryden comes in for yet more criticism before Collier produces a number of specific criticisms of the way the playwrights treat the aristocracy:

> Here we shall find them extremely free and familiar. They dress up the Lords in nicknames, and expose them in characters of contempt. Lord Froth [in *The Double Dealer*] is explained a "solemn coxcomb"; and Lord Rake and Lord Foplington [sic - Collier repeatedly refers to Vanbrugh's Lord Foppington as Foplington] give you their talent in their title. Lord Plausible, in *The Plain Dealer*, acts a ridiculous part, but is withall very civil. He tells Manly "he never attempted to abuse any person." The other [Captain Manly] answers, "What! You were afraid?" Manly goes on, and declares "he would call a rascal by no other title, though his father had left him a duke's". That is, he would call a Duke a rascal. This, I confess, is very much 'plain dealing'.

Collier has made a joke!

Collier continues:

> Such freedoms would appear but oddly in life, especially without provocation. I must own the poet to be an author of good sense. But

under favour, these jests, if we may call them so, are somewhat high seasoned. The humour seems overstrained and the character pushed too far. To proceed [Collier turns his attention to Dryden's *Don Sebastian*]: Mustapha was selling Don Alvarez for a slave. The merchant asks what virtues he has. Mustapha replies, "Virtues, quoth I! He is of a great family and rich, what other virtues would'st thou have in a nobleman?" Don Carlos in [Dryden's] *Love Triumphant*, stands for a gentleman and a man of sense, and out-throws Mustapha a bar's length. He tells us nature has given Sancho "an empty noddle, but Fortune in revenge has filled his pockets; just a Lord's estate in land and wit." This is a handsome compliment to the nobility! And my Lord Salisbury had no doubt of it a good bargain of the dedication. Teresa's general description of a countess [Collier is now referring to D'Urfey's *Don Quixote*] is considerable in its kind. But only 'tis in no condition to appear. In [Vanburgh's] *Relapse*, Sir Tunbelly, who had mistaken young Fashion for Lord Foplington, was afterwards undeceived and before the surprise was quite over, puts the question, "Is it then possible that this should be the true Lord Foplington at last?" The nobleman removes the scruple with great civility and discretion!

"**Lord Foplington:** Why, what do you see in his face to make you doubt of it? Sir, without presuming to have an extraordinary opinion of my figure, give me leave to tell you, if you had seen as many Lords as I have done, you would not think it impossible a person of a worse taille then mine might be a modern man of quality."

I'm sorry to hear modern quality degenerates so much. But, by the way, these liberties are altogether new. They are unpractised by the Latin comedians, and by the English too till very lately, as *The Plain Dealer* observes. And as for Molière in France, he pretends to fly his satire to higher than a Marquis.

And has our stage a particular privilege? Is their charter enlarged, and are they on the same foot of freedom with the slaves in the *Saturnalia*? Must all men be handled alike? Must their roughness be needs played upon title? And can't they lash the vice without pointing upon the quality?

Collier concludes his attack on Dryden:

If, as Mr Dryden rightly defines it, 'a play ought to be a just image of human nature', why are not the decencies of life observed? . . . What necessity is there to kick the coronets about the stage, and to make a man a Lord, only in order to make him a coxcomb?

He ends his fourth chapter with a mixture of conservative politics and sarcasm:

I hope the poets don't intend to revive the old project of levelling, and vote down the House of Peers [Lords]. In earnest, the playhouse is an admirable school of behaviour! This is their way of managing ceremony, distinguishing degree, and entertaining the boxes! But I shall leave them at present to the enjoyment of their talent, and proceed to another argument.

In his fifth chapter, Collier concentrates on just four plays - Dryden's *Amphitryon* and *King Arthur*, D'Urfey's *Don Quixote* and Vanbrugh's *The Relapse*. He provides a detailed criticism of what he sees as the moral failures of these works. Dryden's *Amphitryon*, for example, is not attacked or criticised, as it might be with some justification, for its loose construction, but because Collier insists Dryden is satirising God by presenting Jupiter, the lord of creation in Latin mythology, as an unexalted and by no means blameless character. "To mix Christian and heathen story," says Collier forgetting his own earlier critical methods, "is to imply that one is no more worthy of belief than the other."

Don Quixote is condemned for D'Urfey's "horrible prophaneness", "his want of modesty and regard to the audience", but it is *The Relapse* by Vanbrugh which gains the severest criticism. Collier's attack on Vanbrugh is perhaps the most precisely written section of the *Short View* and the part which attracted most attention - not least from Vanbrugh. For these reasons it is quoted more or less in full in Chapter Five of this book.

The last chapter of the *Short View* is concerned with Collier's opinions of the ways the state and church are presented on stage:

Having in the foregoing chapters discovered some part of the disorders of the English stage; I shall in this last, present the reader with a short view of the sense of antiquity, to which I shall add some modern authorities; from all which it shall appear that plays have generally been looked on as the nurseries of vice, the corrupters of youth, and the grievance of the country where they are suffered.

For much of his book so far, Collier has damned the stage for failing to achieve what he stated was its business: to recommend virtue and discountenance vice. Now he changes tack and damns the stage for itself - apparently advocating the closure of all play-houses. For several pages, he lists such quotations as "plays raise passions and pervert the use of them" - Plato; "the law ought to forbid young people the seeing of comedies" - Aristotle; and similar strictures from other classical authorities such as Cicero, Livy and Tacitus. He quotes, with approval, a long order by a Bishop of Arras forbidding the performance of plays in his diocese, denying burial or administration of the sacraments to any players "unless they shall repent of their crime". Finally, Collier quotes many Christian writers, including Tertullian, St Chrysostom and St Augustine, censuring the stage. His religious authorities all come from the first eight hundred years of Christianity, a period Collier believed to be free of any "corruption".

In a short conclusion he repeats his arguments. It now becomes clear that his real ambition is indeed not censorship of a licentious style of drama (Restoration comedy) but the closure of all theatres:

> Nothing can be more disserviceable to probity and religion, than the management of the stage. It . . . rewards those vices, which 'tis the business of reason to discountenance, . . . it spoils good education . . . and what is still worse, the mischief spreads daily . . . They [the playwrights] have the least pretence to favour, and the most need of repentance, of all men living.

Then comes his unambiguous advice: "My conclusion is, let no-body go to the infamous playhouse." And, lest his warning fails to strike home, Collier repeats his accusations:

> It strikes at the root of principle, draws off the inclinations from virtue, and spoils good education: 'tis the most effectual means to baffle the force of discipline, to emasculate people's spirits, and debauch their manners.

He reaches a climax with a typical series of staccato, rhetorical questions:

> How many of the unwary have these Syrens devoured? And how often has the best blood been tainted with this infection? What disappointment of parents, what confusion in families, and what beggary in estates have been hence occasioned?

The stage, he finally concludes, is an illness which infects good families and leads to family break-ups and poverty. He has a

further pessimistic diagnosis of this moral malady: the hopeless-
ness of a cure when the victim or patient is happy to be infected:

> The fever works up toward madness, and will scarcely endure to be
> touched. And what hope is there of health when the patient strikes in
> with the disease, and flies in the face of the remedy. Can religion
> retrieve us? Yes, when we don't despise it. But while our notions are
> naught, our lives will hardly be otherwise . . . You may almost as well
> feed a man without a mouth, as give advice where there's no disposi-
> tion to receive it.

Such then, in outline, is Collier's argument as he expressed it in
the first of his forays against the stage. As we shall see, it provoked
a fiery, intemperate and enjoyable debate over the following months
and years. It is also worth noting that it was followed by a simmer-
ing debate over the next two centuries in which literary historians
wrangled about the value and credibility of Collier's attack and
about the amount of influence he has had on English stage history.
There has even been disagreement as to the precise object of his
censure and of his primary purpose. Was it reform or abolition of
the playhouses? Was his principal target the playwrights or was the
Short View a coded attack on the Court itself or society at large? It
has been suggested variously that he saw himself as a dramatic
critic, as a priest, or as a propagandist on behalf of James II. Others
have dismissed him as a blatant controversialist who enjoyed a
good row and was simply courting notoriety in the hope of gaining
fame and money. He was also accused of looking for dirt, and
finding it, whether it existed or not.

J. E. Spingarn, writing in his once definitive *Critical Essays of the
Seventeenth Century*, considered Collier to be:

> . . . principally a moralist, but [he] borrowed some of his weapons
> from the literary critics, and indeed based some of his arguments on
> purely critical grounds.

Certainly, the controversy that followed the appearance of the *Short
View* revolved around the question whether it was indeed "the
business of plays is to recommend virtue and discountenance
vice". As Ben Jonson had asked, to Collier's subsequent approval,
was it indeed "the office of a comic poet to imitate justice and
instruct to life?"

It must be stressed that, in attempting to reform the stage and convert the wits, Collier took as his authorities the dramatists of earlier periods, rather than attempting a narrowly theological argument as he might well have done. It is also evident he had read widely, if not always with any subtle dramatic appreciation. He was a fervent polemicist, convinced of the value of every reform of which he was advocate. Macaulay properly described him "as a great master of sarcasm, a great master of rhetoric". Logic and objectivity might have been greater assets.

For what blunted his case was Collier's frequent inability to distinguish between representation and reality, between art and life and between satire and an object of satire. In the *Short View*, he regularly assumes that a dramatist who depicts successful rakes must be a rake himself. For example, he cannot see Foppington as an object for Vanbrugh's ridicule, nor realise that an artist may paint a vice in order to damn it. Whether the Restoration playwrights did regard the follies of their characters as vices is debatable. They certainly assumed extra-marital sexual experience, for men if not for all women, as a fact of life. Their male characters prospered, despite their licentiousness and they were often rewarded with rich heiresses in the fifth act.

It must be said that the playhouse was indeed a place of "immorality and profaneness". By the time Etherege had written his last play (1676), Restoration comedy was built firmly upon certain stock characters and situations. In it, marriage is a joke; sexual permissiveness is not only prevalent but the rule; and the hero must be a rake, especially in the plays of Vanbrugh and Farquhar. Etherege's *The Man of Mode* is the picture of a diverting fop. Dorimant "is simultaneously casting off one mistress . . . seducing another, and courting a third." In his opening speech, he moans about the dullness of a love letter written "after the heat of the business is over". It is not difficult to hear the laughter of recognition from the male chauvinist rakes in the audience.

Some playwrights did "aim to mend". Wycherley is considered by some to be guided by moral principles. Dryden expressed the need for moral order even if, as a professional writer, he also felt he had to give the public what it wanted. Similarly, in his early plays, Shadwell presents us with various serious young lovers and protested against "the bawdy and the repartee". But by 1672, he too had acquiesced with dramatic fashion. *Epsom Wells* has its fair share of rakes and cuckolds. In fact, Doctor Johnson very fairly epitomised the Restoration dramatists when he wrote:

> Themselves they studied, as they felt they write:
> Intrigue was plot, obscenity was wit.
> Vice always found a sympathetic friend;
> They pleased their age, and did not aim to mend.

Had Collier been so succinct, there might have been no controversy and no reform. What made him controversial was his undiscriminating fury, his readiness to detect allusions where none were present, especially when dealing with profanity; and, not least, his sensitivity to any possible insult to the cloth. He consequently emerges as an authoritarian censor wanting to see nothing but virtue upon stage with every vice condemned and the perpetrator punished. He also proves himself devoid of any sense of humour - to the delight of his detractors.

J. W. Krutch, while admitting that he was "essentially narrow-minded", can also see what it was about Collier that won him a hearing despite his bombast:

> His earnestness was one great asset, his style another. To the modern ear the latter is sometimes offensive, but it was admirably in the tradition of seventeenth century controversy. His contemporaries liked learning and liked raillery. Collier appealed to both these traits by mixing a bewildering number of citations, pertinent and impertinent, with sneers, taunts and irony, together with exuberant raillery and abuse.

4

The Critics Answer Back

According to Allardyce Nicholl, in *A History of Restoration Drama*, Collier was at one time held to be almost wholly responsible for the "violent revulsion of feeling with regard to contemporary comedy." Professor Krutch also suggests that Collier was "responsible largely for the orthodox views of the eighteenth and nineteenth centuries" and for transforming "a brilliant and immoral tradition into a dull and moral one." These twentieth century commentators were stating nothing new. Two hundred years earlier, the critic Tom Davies, in his *Dramatic Miscellanies*, had stated roundly: "The physic he administered was so powerful, that a sudden and almost effectual reformation took place." The following century, the historian Macaulay gave Collier his best notice:

A great and rapid reform in all departments of our lighter literature was the effect of his labours; for to his eloquence and courage is to be chiefly ascribed the purification of our lighter literature from that foul taint which had been contracted during the anti-puritan reactions.

But, as we have seen, Collier was only part of a growing trend. Evelyn, Blackmore and Gould had penned criticisms of the stage. In 1694, one Joseph Wright, in his *Country Conversations*, had complained of stage attacks on the clergy. The Court was now more Calvinist than Catholic. City values were being expressed more vocally. The decade saw the foundation of the Society for the Reformation of Manners which attacked the playhouses in 1694. Between 1696 and 1698 several writs and proclamations were issued against swearing and other forms of immorality, as presented on the London stage. About this time the first newspapers were appearing and, through their columns, the inhabitants of London were beginning to express their support for reform. In the subsequent war of pamphlets, opinions were to be expressed in print in many cities, including Bath and Edinburgh. It was, however, as yet a smouldering discussion. Then, in 1698, Collier not only lit the match but doused it liberally with his inflammatory arguments - thus creating a blazing, high-temperature bonfire.

Yet the success of the *Short View* was not merely due to its author's rhetoric or to the fact that Collier articulated what growing numbers had been thinking in the past few years. Yes, Collier was "in the swim" of middle-class reforming zeal, as K. M. P. Burton of the University of Nottingham suggested in 1961, but he was also, in modern terms, a celebrity. He was still an outlaw, with no legal right to be in London. He was an outcast from his calling, yet he still considered himself a priest and practised as one. And here in the *Short View*, he revealed himself publicly as an informed observer of the London scene, boldly attacking the favoured writers of Charles II and James II.

As a result of the subsequent outcry and arguments, King William issued a solemn proclamation "against vice and profaneness of all sorts" and granted Collier a Royal Pardon. The Church of England asked Collier to consider returning to the fold, since he was now respectable. He remained faithful to his non-juring principles, but gathered many other allies. These ranged from extreme Puritans, who wished to see the drama abolished, to the purists of dramatic theory, and the moderate middle-classes.

But he also incurred the fury of the dramatists and some influential critics. Alarmed at the publicity and swing of public opinion, they wrote not so much in their own defence, but rather to show the absurdities and inconsistencies of Collier's attack. Collier and his supporters responded and the result was the splendid pamphlet war that has come to be known as the 'Collier Controversy' of which J. W. Krutch takes a somewhat partial overview:

48

He called forth a great and very miscellaneous company of wits, critics, philosophers, and fanatics who fell upon one another in a most undignified battle-royal through which no one really distinguished himself except Collier.

He also makes a much fairer point about the debate:

To mention in chronological order all the contributions to the controversy or to balance reply and counter-reply would be tedious, and since there is endless repetition, uninstructive.

With that excuse, what follows is a selective survey of the some forty pamphlets, articles, essays and prefaces that resulted directly from the publication of the *Short View*.

The first known reply is that of the playwright Charles Gildon. In the printed preface to his play *Phaeton: or The Fatal Divorce* (published on April 30 1698) he admits the "indecencies" of the English stage but asserts "the wit of man can invent no way so efficacious as dramatic poetry to advance virtue and wisdom". This short preface is, however, most notable for Gildon's repeated assertions that he will return to the attack during the coming summer. Whether various subsequent and anonymous pamphlets were his work is unproven.

Around this time, the text of a play by Peter Motteux was published. Motteux was a Frenchman living in London and editor of the *Gentleman's Journal* which may be described fairly as one of the first magazines. His play was called *Beauty in Distress* and for its publication he provided a preface in which he quoted French religious authorities in order to argue that, while drama may be corrupt, it was not intrinsically evil. More interestingly, his book included a *Poetical Epistle to Motteux* by Dryden.

In its opening lines, Dryden refers to the attacks on the stage by Blackmore and Collier - clearly suggesting that the arts of poetry and drama have divine approval:

'Tis hard, my friend, to write in such an age,
As damns not only poets, but the stage.
That sacred art, by Heav'n itself infus'd,
Which Moses, David, Solomon have us'd
Is now to be no more.

Dryden goes on to gently suggest that Collier overstated his case:

> Were they content to prune the lavish vine
> Of straggling branches, and improve the wine,
> Who but a mad man would his faults defend?
> All would submit; for all but fools will mend . . .

However, he then admits his own regret at having written anything that might be considered profane:

> What I have loosely or profanely writ,
> Let them to fires (their due desert) commit.

Significantly, Dryden made no attempt here to disprove the many charges of immodesty and profanity laid against his own plays by Collier - despite the strength of Collier's personal attack. As Sister Rose Anthony puts it:

> Collier had dared to attack Dryden; had dared to call in question the morality of his plays; had dared to censure certain literary principles of the 'Father of our Modern Drama'. He had dared to attack him - not once but many times throughout the *Short View*, and to attack caustically. Those who were acquainted with Dryden, those who remembered his controversies with Howard, with Shadwell, and with Shaftesbury expected a sharp reply. More than once Dryden had used his pen to paint an ignominious picture of him who had aroused his ire . . . but Dryden was silent. This silence chafed the less gifted of the playwrights and angered those more capable of satiric rejoiner; it mystified his friends and confused his enemies.

In July of that summer, the playwright Thomas D'Urfey articulated this confusion and concern:

> I could have wished one who is best able, and whose admirable genius and skill in poetry would have been remarkably serviceable, had drawn his pen to defend the rights of the stage, though he had owned the loosenesses of it.

Another anonymous writer complained thus of Dryden's failure to savage Collier:

> Where Mr Collier made so vigorous an attack upon our stages as shook the foundation; what was the reason, in so desperate a juncture... that only the *minor* poets appeared? Where was the great master of the muses and father of our modern drama?

Much later, Samuel Johnson was to offer a possible explanation of Dryden's failure to enter wholeheartedly into the debate: "His conscience or his prudence withheld him from the conflict."

50

Meanwhile, those "minor poets" had not been silent. A week or so after Motteux's play was printed, there appeared a twenty-two-page anonymous pamphlet *A Letter to A. H. Esq.: Concerning the Stage*. Judging from its tone, it seems likely that its author had studied Collier's arguments carefully and was a friend of the playwrights:

> But what can Mr Collier mean by exposing the stage so? He would not surely have it silenced. That would be a little too barbarous, and too much like cant to be entertained by men of thought or ingenuity.

The writer goes on to argue in defence of a regulated stage and states that the immorality of the age is not the fault of the playhouse. He then attempts to answer Collier's more significant arguments, frequently lauding Dryden while questioning the literary value and morality of D'Urfey's plays. Unlike many of those who attacked Collier that summer, he defends the playwrights for satirising the clergy:

> Who can believe that when Mr Vanbrugh disguises a parson, that he thought of these men, or any who lives soberly, and make religion their business, and at the same time, don't make it inconsistent with good manners?

More pamphlets and papers were published that month (May 1698) and then on May 26 there appeared a lengthier, if not more substantial, contribution to the debate. This was the 118-page anonymous *Defence of Dramatic Poetry Being a Review of Mr Collier's View of the Immorality and Profaneness of the Stage*. Its preface includes a jibe at Collier for being a Non-juror and therefore unemployed:

> It had been an infinite higher glory, both to the book and the author, had the argument been taken up in his pulpit reign. Then he would have convinced the world that he put pen to paper in the spirit of zeal and piety, and not left himself open to that untoward suspicion, viz. that all this laboured pile of stage-reformation is only the product of idleness and abdication.

Rather more fairly, the writer points out Collier's shift between his first and final chapters from arguing for the reformation of the stage towards his call for its abolition:

> For here he throws by the pruning hook, and takes up the axe. In due prevention, therefore against so dangerous a weapon, in so angry a hand, we'll endeavour first to guard the root.

While this anonymous defender of the stage has some pleasantly colloquial asides - "Good heaven! How perversely does this angry gentleman scribble!" - it has to be admitted that his 118 pages are somewhat verbose. A week later (June 6), a much more significant defence was to appear.

John Dennis was born in 1657, was educated at Harrow and then at Collier's college, Caius, Cambridge just after Collier had graduated. He wrote a number of tragedies, later to be damned by Alexander Pope, but is chiefly remembered for his critical works. His *The Usefulness of the Stage, To the Happiness of Mankind, To Government, and To Religion* is, in the words of Sister Rose Anthony, "the most learned, the most systematic and the most compelling of the contemporary replies", though she also suggests "the essay makes heavy reading today." In his reply, Dennis writes:

> This little treatise was conceived, disposed, transcribed and printed in a month; and though on that very account it may not be wholly free from error, yet this I can assure the reader, that I have industriously endeavoured not to err, though I verily believe that Mr Collier industriously endeavoured to err, as far as he thought it might be consistent with the deceiving of others.

In other words, he believed Collier was unscrupulous. However, he did not set out to answer Collier's points one by one, nor even chapter by chapter. Rather, his overriding purpose is to prove the usefulness of the stage. In his introduction, he demonstrated that Collier himself began by arguing for stage reform, so that it might serve Collier's purpose as defined in the opening sentence of the *Short View*, but then went on to contradict himself by concluding that the stage should be abolished:

> My business therefore is a vindication of the stage and not of the corruptions or the abuses of it. And therefore, I have no further meddled with Mr Collier's book, than as I have had occasion to shew, that he has endeavoured to make some things pass for abuses, either of the stage in general, or of the English stage particularly, which are so far from being abuses, that they may be accounted excellences.

He concludes his introduction with a reprimand to Collier for his lack of "either the meekness of a true Christian or the humility of an exemplary pastor" and regrets acidly that Collier has:

neither the reasoning of a man of sense . . . nor the style of a polite man, nor the sincerity of an honest man, nor the humanity of a gentleman, or a man of letters.

His main argument is that the theatre tends to happiness which he equates with pleasure and defines pleasure as the consequence of "passion". Philosopher that he was, he saw that the fundamental question of the acceptability of pleasure was the controversy. For his part, Dennis insists that happiness and pleasure-seeking are not, in themselves, evil. The theatre, he argues, arouses the passions, the sole source of pleasure; and lasting pleasure can only be obtained from passions which do not conflict with reason: what he described as "the virtuous passions". He continues by observing that pleasure may, itself, be of positive value - something Collier was unlikely ever to admit. With some humour, doubtless lost on Collier, Dennis shows the dangers of quoting the classical masters. He concedes to Collier that Ovid said the theatre was the best place to find a mistress. He then asks Collier if he noticed that Ovid said the second-best place was the temple or church. Attacks of morality may kill, he added, but they cannot create.

The second part of his pamphlet aims to prove that the stage is useful to government and, somewhat idiosyncratically, to the English government in particular:

Now there is no nation in Europe, as has been observed above a thousand times, that is so generally addicted to the spleen as the English . . . Now the English being more splenetic than any other people, and consequently more thoughtful and more reflecting . . . it follows that the English to be happy have more need than other people of something that will raise their passions in such a manner, as shall be agreeable to their reasons, and that by consequence they have more need of the drama.

Or as he puts it later:

Drama may be said to be instrumental in a peculiar manner to the welfare of the English Government; because there is no people on the face of the Earth so prone to rebellion as the English, or so apt to quarrel among themselves.

Despite such debatable points, his pamphlet was a far better argued defence of the stage than any that had previously appeared. Its tone may be hostile to Collier and, in the light of his subsequent defences of the stage, it can be argued that Dennis had a personal aversion to the author of the *Short View* but, in the words of J. W. Krutch:

> It does considerable credit to the perspicacity of John Dennis that he saw more clearly than anyone else that such ideas lay at the back of even Collier's mind . . . Dennis saw that there was involved a fundamental question of the value of pleasure, and he set himself to formulate a moral but anti-ascetic philosophy. He maintains that pleasure is not in itself an evil, but that mankind lives for happiness. And happiness, he says, is concerned with the passions and comes only through such exercise of them as does not result in a conflict with the will . . . Drama arouses the rational passions, and is therefore useful to the happiness of mankind. A man who is familiar with the theatre is less easily moved than one who is not, and therefore to say that the drama unduly stimulates the passions is false, for the theatregoer is less likely than another to be swept away by irrational emotion.

Nor, according to Krutch, does Dennis duck the question whether a play can encourage immoral behaviour: "Only a bad play will encourage lawless love, but to encourage virtuous love is to perform a service rather than, as some would have it, to stimu-late a vice." Two days after the appearance of Dennis's pamphlet, the first of the playwrights to answer Collier published his self-vindication.

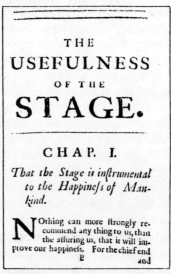

Figure 3: *The Usefulness of the Stage*

5

The Attack on Vanbrugh

The play which most attracted Collier's ire was Vanbrugh's *The Relapse*. "I almost wonder the smoke of it has not darkened the sun and turned the air to poison," he wrote with characteristic rhetoric. Indeed, a major part of the fifth chapter of the *Short View* is one sustained denunciation of the play whilst also being one of Collier's more cogent and interesting passages. For once, he attempts to reason from dramatic values. He tries to show that the plot is ill-contrived, the manners or characters are not credible - that is, a marquis does not behave as a marquis should; a lady is not always typical of her class - and that the dramatic unities are broken. He again stresses the importance of decorum - the dramatic convention that, for example, an old man must be feeble:

> To manage otherwise is to desert nature; and makes the play appear monstrous and chimerical. So that instead of an image of life, 'tis rather an image of impossibility.

The Relapse was Vanbrugh's first performed play, written in a hurry to capitalise on the success of Colley Cibber's *Love's Last Shift* to which it is, in effect, a sequel. Vanbrugh borrowed Cibber's pivotal character, Sir Novelty Fashion, but elevated him to the peerage as Lord Foppington. The play had its première at Drury Lane late in November 1696. It is therefore perverse of the *Cambridge History of English Literature* to

55

accuse Vanbrugh of, or indeed to praise him for, making "no conces-
sions" to Collier - it was to be nearly eighteen months before Vanbrugh
might have read the *Short View*.

Collier includes in his attack a brief synopsis of the play. For readers
unfamiliar with it, a slightly fuller summary of its two plots might be
helpful: Loveless and his wife Amanda have returned to London from
the country. Amanda correctly fears the attractions of the town will
lead her husband astray. He falls for a woman he has seen at the theatre.
She is none other than Amanda's widowed cousin Berinthia. Unaware
of her husband's interest, Amanda asks Berinthia to stay with them.
Berinthia is attracted to Loveless.

Loveless's friend Worthy (a former lover of Berinthia) sets his sights
on Amanda. Worthy and Berinthia agree to work together to seduce
husband and wife. Loveless has little trouble in seducing Berinthia,
whilst Amanda continues to suspect her husband of being interested
in an unknown woman. When Berinthia proves he has been unfaith-
ful, Amanda considers revenge. Worthy steps forward as a possible
lover but Amanda remains "firm in her virtue".

The second or sub-plot concerns Sir Novelty Fashion who has just
bought himself the title of Lord Foppington and is concerned only with
being fashionable. He is about to marry Miss Hoyden, the daughter of
Sir Tunbelly Clumsey, a widowed country squire. This does not stop
Foppington from paying court to Amanda. Foppington's younger
brother, Tom Fashion, returns from the continent penniless. Lord
Foppington has little interest in helping him. Coupler, a professional
matchmaker and homosexual, offers, for a fee, to help him go down to
the country under Lord Foppington's name and to steal the elder
brother's bride plus her fortune. Fashion achieves this, marrying Miss
Hoyden secretly with the help of her nurse and corruptible chaplain.
Lord Foppington arrives too late, is imprisoned as an impostor and
only gains his freedom thanks to an old friend, Sir John Friendly. Tom
Fashion escapes. Miss Hoyden agrees to a second marriage with Lord
Foppington but, on everyone's return to London, Fashion produces
chaplain and nurse as his witnesses. Foppington admits defeat.

So does the story offend against morality? Is immorality rewarded?
Certainly Loveless betrays Amanda, but he is presented as an obvi-

ously weak character whose name indicates his nature. It can be argued that, although cuckolded, Amanda has lost nothing since Loveless was never worth having. Indeed, Amanda emerges with some considerable dignity. Berinthia, who behaves quite selfishly in encouraging and accepting Loveless, can be said to have got the man she deserves. Loveless, for his part, is likely to continue his philandering ways.

In the sub-plot, spendthrift young Tom Fashion betrays his brother by deceitfully marrying Hoyden and is rewarded by Vanbrugh for his pains. Yet he can be played as the victim of primogeniture whereby a father's money went mainly to the older son. Additionally, Lord Foppington, who is obviously having a love affair with himself, can be said to have no need of Miss Hoyden or her money. As J. W. Krutch succinctly puts it: "As for putting the prize in the wrong hand, Sir Foppington is a heartless and brainless ass." What's more, Fashion and Hoyden seem to accept each other on sight: they seem to be at least compatible if not truly in love. Collier however concludes that the moral this plot teaches is "that all younger brothers should be careful to run out their fortunes as fast, and as ill, as they can."

Nevertheless, Collier was not the only one to attack Vanbrugh as an immoral writer who celebrates "uninhibited indulgence of physical appetite." In the 1770s the play was thought to be in need of bowdlerisation. Sheridan, for one, reworked it as *A Trip to Scarborough*. It is only in recent years that the original play has regained popularity, partly because the new permissiveness has made it once again acceptable fun. Bernard Harris, in his introduction to the New Mermaid edition of the play, provides a more critical defence against the charge of naughtiness:

Vanbrugh's opinion of humanity is an exuberant compound of cynicism and generosity, and possibly his own standpoint is nearest to that displayed by Worthy; self-interest is usually uppermost, but it has a capacity to acknowledge higher values and to give way.

Collier damns Vanbrugh, as we shall see, for writing bawdy, blasphemous and dramatically incompetent plays. Harris, for one, defends Vanbrugh on the third charge:

The great strength of *The Relapse* lies in the play's sheer vivacity, whether in language or action. Its dialogue is written with natural ease, and though it lacks the intellectual wit of many comedies of manners, this is partly because, Foppington apart, it is less concerned with affectations of behaviour than with naturalness of character.

These were not qualities Collier appreciated nor could he see that Lord Foppington's affectations are an object of ridicule and satire. When the would-be beau complained he was bored on Sundays, Collier took it in deadly earnest and believed it blasphemy.

What follows is the third section of the fifth chapter of the *Short View* and is subtitled "Remarks upon *The Relapse*". Note that, even when damning the immorality of the characters, Collier relies not on the Bible as his authority but on the critics Rapin and Rymer. This, along with his attack on the play's construction, suggests that Collier felt this was the way to win converts from what he saw as the wicked world of the playhouse. It has already been pointed out that he wrote "Lovelace" for Loveless and "Foplington" for Foppington. The correct names have been reinstated here.

Because this author swaggers so much in his preface, and seems to look big upon his performance, I shall spend a few more thoughts than ordinary upon his play, and examine it briefly in the fable, the moral, the characters, etc. The fable I take to be as follows:

Fashion, a lewd, prodigal younger brother, is reduced to extremity. Upon his arrival from his travels, he meets with Coupler, an old sharping matchmaker. This man puts him upon a project of cheating his elder brother, Lord Foppington, of a rich fortune. Young Fashion, being refused a sum of money by his brother, goes into Coupler's plot, bubbles Sir Tunbelly of his daughter, and makes himself master of a fair estate.

From the form and constitution of the fable, I observe first that there is a misnomer in the title. The play should not have been called *The Relapse: or Virtue in Danger* [Vanbrugh's subtitle]. Loveless and Amanda, from whose characters these names are drawn, are persons of inferior consideration. Loveless sinks in the middle of the fourth act, and we hear no more of him till towards the end of the fifth where he enters once more, but then 'tis as Cato did the Senate house, only to go out again. And as for Amanda, she has nothing to do but to stand a shock of courtship, and carry off her virtue. This, I confess, is a great task in the playhouse but no main matter in the play.

The intrigue and the discovery, the great revolution and success, turns upon Young Fashion. He, without competition, is the principal person in the comedy. And therefore 'The Younger Brother' or 'The Fortunate Cheat', had been much a more proper name. Now when a poet can't rig out a title page, 'tis but a bad sign of his holding out to the epilogue.

Secondly, I observe the moral is vicious: it points the wrong way, and puts the prize into the wrong hand. It seems to make lewdness the reason of desert, and gives Young Fashion a second fortune, only for debauching away his first. A short view of his character will make good this reflection. To begin with him: he confesses himself a rake, swears and blasphemes, curses and challenges his elder brother, cheats him of his mistress, and gets him laid by the heels in a dog-kennel. And what was the ground of all this unnatural quarrelling and outrage? Why, the main of it was only because Lord Foppington refused to supply his luxury and make good his extravagance. This Young Fashion, after all, is the poet's man of merit. He provides a plot and a fortune on purpose for him. To speak freely, a lewd character seldom wants good luck in comedy. So that whenever you see a thorough libertine, you may always swear he is in a rising way, and that the poet intends to make him a great man. In short, this play perverts the end of comedy: which, as Monsieur Rapin observes, ought to regard reformation and public improvement. But the Relapser [Vanbrugh] had a more fashionable fancy in his head. His moral holds forth this notable instruction:

First, that all younger brothers should be careful to run out their circumstances as fast and as ill as they can. And when they have put their affairs in this posture of advantage, they may conclude themselves in the high road to wealth and success. For, as Fashion blasphemously applies it, 'Providence takes care of men of merit.'

Secondly, that when a man is pressed, his business is not to be governed by scruples, or formalise upon conscience and honesty. The quickest expedients are the best; for in such cases the occasion justifies the means, and a knight of the post [a man who has stood in the pillory] is as good as one of the Garter. In the third place, it may not be improper to look a little into the plot. Here the poet ought to play the politician if ever. This part should have some strokes of conduct and strains of invention more then ordinary. There should be something that is admirable and unexpected to surprise the audience. And all this finess [artfulness] must work by gentle degrees, by a due preparation of incidents, and by instruments which are probable. 'Tis Mr Rapin's remark that without probability 'everything is lame and faulty'. Where there is no pretence to miracle and machine, matters must not exceed the force of belief. To produce effects without proportion and likelihood in the cause is farce and magic, and

59

looks more like conjuring than conduct. Let us examine the Relapser by these rules. To discover his plot, we must lay open somewhat more of the fable:

Lord Foppington, a town beau, had agreed to marry the daughter of Sir Tunbelly Clumsey, a country gentleman, who lived fifty miles from London. Notwithstanding this small distance, the Lord had never seen his mistress, nor the knight his son-in-law. Both parties, out of their great wisdom, leave the treating the match to Coupler. When all the preliminaries of settlement were adjusted, and Lord Foppington expected by Sir Tunbelly in a few days, Coupler betrays his trust to Young Fashion. He advises him to go down before his brother; to counterfeit his person, and pretend that the strength of his inclinations brought him thither before his time and without his retinue. And to make him pass upon Sir Tunbelly, Coupler gives him his letter, which was to be Lord Foppington's credential. Young Fashion, thus provided, posts down to Sir Tunbelly, is received for Lord Foppington, and by the help of a little folly and knavery in the family marries the young lady without her father's knowledge and a week before the appointment.

This is the main of the contrivance. The counterturn in Lord Foppington's appearing afterwards, and the support of the main plot by Bull's and Nurse's attesting the marriage, contains little of moment. And here we may observe that Lord Foppington has an unlucky disagreement in his character. This misfortune sits hard upon the credibility of the design. 'Tis true he was formal and fantastic, smitten with dress and equipage, and it may be vapoured by his perfumes; but his behaviour is far from that of an idiot. This being granted, 'tis very unlikely this Lord, with his five thousand pounds per annum, should leave the choice of his mistress to Coupler, and take her person and fortune upon content. To court thus blindfold and by proxy does not agree with the method of estate nor the niceness of a beau. However, the poet makes him engage hand over head, without so much as the sight of her picture. His going down to Sir Tunbelly was as extraordinary as his courtship. He had never seen this gentleman. He must know him to be beyond measure suspicious, and there was no admittance without Coupler's letter. This letter, which was the key to the castle, he forgot to take with him, and tells you 'twas stolen by his brother Tam [sic]. And for his part he neither had the discretion to get another, nor yet to produce that written by him to Sir Tunbelly. Had common sense been consulted upon this occasion, the plot had been at an end, and the play had sunk in the fourth act. The remainder subsists purely upon the strength of folly, and of folly altogether improbable and out of character. The salvo of Sir John Friendly's appearing at last and vouching for Lord Foppington won't mend the matter. For, as the story informs us, Lord Foppington never depended on this reserve: he knew nothing of this gentleman being in the country, nor where he lived. The truth is, Sir John was left in town, and the Lord had neither concerted his journey with him nor engaged his assistance.

Let us now see how Sir Tunbelly hangs together. This gentleman the poet makes a Justice of the Peace and a Deputy Lieutenant, and seats him fifty miles from London: but by his character you would take him for one of Hercules's monsters, or some giant in *Guy of Warwick* [a fourteenth century verse romance]. His behaviour is altogether romance, and has nothing agreeable to time or country. When Fashion and Lory [his servant] went down, they find the bridge drawn up, the gates barred, and the blunderbuss cocked at the first civil question. And when Sir Tunbelly had notice of this formidable appearance, he sallies out with the posse of the family, and marches against a couple of strangers with a life guard of halberds, scythes, and pitchforks. And to make sure work, young Hoyden is locked up at the first approach of the enemy. Here you have prudence and wariness to the excess of fable and frenzy. And yet this mighty man of suspicion trusts Coupler with the disposal of his only daughter, and his estate into the bargain.

And what was this Coupler? Why, a sharper by character, and little better by profession. Farther: Lord Foppington and the Knight are but a day's journey asunder, and yet by their treating by proxy and commission one would fancy a dozen degrees of latitude betwixt them. And as for Young Fashion, excepting Coupler's letter, he has all imaginable marks of imposture upon him. He comes before his time and without the retinue expected, and has nothing of the air of Lord Foppington's conversation. When Sir Tunbelly asked him, 'Pray where are your coaches and servants, my Lord?', he makes a trifling excuse: 'Sir, that I might give you and your fair daughter a proof how impatient I am to be nearer akin to you, I left my equipage to follow me, and came away post, with only one servant.' To be in such a hurry of inclination for a person he never saw is somewhat strange! Besides, 'tis very unlikely Lord Foppington should hazard his complexion on horseback, outride his figure, and appear a bridegroom in déshabillé. You may as soon persuade a peacock out of his train as a beau out of his equipage, especially upon such an occasion. Lord Foppington would scarcely speak to his brother, just come ashore, till the grand committee of tailors, seamstresses etc, was dispatched.

Pomp and curiosity were this Lord's inclination; why then should he mortify without necessity, make his first approaches thus out of form, and present himself to his mistress at such disadvantage? And as this is the character of Lord Foppington, so 'tis reasonable to suppose Sir Tunbelly acquainted with it. An enquiry into the humour and management of a son-in-law is very natural and customary. So that we can't without violence to sense suppose Sir Tunbelly a stranger to Lord Foppington's singularities. These reasons were enough in all conscience to make Sir Tunbelly suspect a juggle, and that Fashion was no better than a counterfeit. Why then was the credential swallowed without chewing; why was not Hoyden locked up, and a pause made for farther enquiry? Did this justice never hear of such a thing as knavery, or had he ever greater reason to guard against it? More wary steps might well have been expected from Sir Tunbelly. To run from one extreme of caution to another of credulity is highly improbable. In short, either Lord Foppington and Sir Tunbelly are fools, or they are not. If they are, where lies the cunning in over-reaching them? What conquest can there be without opposition? If they are not fools, why does the poet make them so? Why is their conduct so gross, so parti-coloured, and inconsistent? Take them either way, and the plot miscarries. The first supposition makes it dull, and the later, incredible. So much for the plot. I shall now in the fourth place touch briefly upon the manners.

The manners, in the language of the stage, have a signification somewhat particular. Aristotle and Rapin call them the causes and principles of action. They are formed upon the diversities of age and sex, of fortune, capacity, and education. The propriety of manners consists in a conformity of practise and principle, of nature and behaviour. For the purpose: an old man must not appear with the profuseness and levity of youth; a gentleman must not talk like a clown, nor a country girl like a town jilt [harlot]. And when the characters are feigned, 'tis Horace's rule to keep them uniform, and consistent, and agreeable to their first setting out. The poet must be careful to hold his persons tight to their calling and pretensions. He must not shift and shuffle their understandings, let them skip from wits to blockheads nor from courtiers to pedants. On the other hand, if their business is playing the fool, keep them strictly to their duty, and never indulge them in fine sentences. To manage otherwise is to desert nature, and makes the play appear monstrous and chimerical. So that instead of an image of life, 'tis rather an image of impossibility. To apply some of these remarks to the Relapser:

The fine Berinthia, one of the top-characters, is impudent and profane. Loveless would engage her secrecy, and bids her swear. She answers, I do:

'**Loveless:** By what?

Berinthia: By woman.

Loveless: That's swearing by my deity; do it by your own, or I shan't believe you.

Berinthia: By man, then.'

This lady promises Worthy her endeavours to corrupt Amanda and then they make a profane jest upon the office. In the progress of the play, after a great deal of lewd discourse with Loveless, Berinthia is carried off into a closet, and lodged in a scene of debauch. Here is decency and reservedness to a great exactness! Monsieur Rapin blames Ariosto and Taco [Italian writers] for representing two of their women over free and airy. These poets, says he, rob women of their character, which is modesty. Mr Rymer is of the same opinion. His words are these:

'Nature knows nothing in the manners which so properly and particularly distinguish a woman as her modesty. An impudent woman is fit only to be kicked and exposed in comedy.'

Now, Berinthia appears in comedy, 'tis true; but neither to be kicked nor exposed. She makes a considerable figure, has good usage, keeps the best company, and goes off without censure or disadvantage.

Let us now take a turn or two with Sir Tunbelly's heiress of £1,500 a year. This young lady swears, talks smut, and is upon the matter just as rag-mannered as *Mary the Buxsome*. 'Tis plain the Relapser copied Mr D'Urfey's original, which is a sign he was somewhat pinched. Now, this character was no great beauty in *Buxsome*; but it becomes the knight's daughter much worse. Buxsome was a poor peasant, which made her rudeness more natural and expected. But Deputy Lieutenant's children don't use to appear with the behaviour of beggars. To breed all people alike, and make no distinction between a seat and a cottage is not over artful, nor very ceremonious to the country gentlemen. The Relapser gives miss a pretty soliloquy; I'll transcribe it for the reader. She swears by her maker [she says "ecod"]:

"'Tis well I have a husband a coming, or I'd marry the baker, I would so! Nobody can knock at the gate, but presently I must be locked up; and here's the young greyhound ***** [Collier does not transcribe the word "bitch"] can run loose about the house all day long, she can, 'tis very well!'

Afterwards her language is too lewd to be quoted. Here is a compound of ill manners and contradiction! Is this a good resemblance of quality, a description of a great heiress, and the effect of a cautious education? By her coarseness you would think her bred upon a common; and by her confidence, in the nursery of the playhouse. I suppose the Relapser fancies that calling her Miss Hoyden [a rude or ill-bred girl] is enough to justify her ill-manners. By his favour, this is a mistake. To represent her thus unhewn, he should have suited her condition to her name a little better. For there is no charm in the words as to matters of breeding: an unfashionable name won't make a man a clown. Education is not formed upon sounds and syllables, but upon circumstances and quality. So that if he was resolved to have shown her thus unpolished, he should have made her keep sheep, or brought her up at the wash-bowl.

Sir Tunbelly accosts young Fashion much at the same rate of accomplishment: 'My Lord, I humbly crave leave to bid you welcome in a cup of sack-wine.' One would imagine the poet was over-dosed before he gave the justice a glass. For sack-wine is too low for a petty constable. This peasantly expression agrees neither with the gentleman's figure nor with the rest of his behaviour. I find we should have a creditable magistracy, if the Relapser had the making them. Here the characters are pinched in sense, and stinted to short allowance. At another time they are over-indulged, and treated above expectation.

For the purpose: vanity and formalising is Lord Foppington's part. To let him speak without awkwardness and affectation is to put him out of his element. There must be gum and stiffening in his discourse to make it natural. However, the Relapser has taken a fancy to his person and given him some of the most genteel raillery in the whole play. To give an instance or two: this Lord, in discourse with Fashion, forgets his name, flies out into sense and smooth expression, out talks his brother and, abating the starched similitude of a watch, discovers nothing of affectation for almost a page together. He relapses into the same intemperance of good sense in an other dialogue between him and his brother. I shall cite a little of it:

'**Young Fashion:** Unless you are so kind to assist me in redeeming my annuity, I know no remedy but to go take a purse.

Lord Foppington: Why, faith, Tam, to give you my sense of the thing, I do think taking a purse the best remedy in the world; for if you succeed, you are relieved that way; if you are taken - you are relieved the other.'

Fashion, being disappointed of a supply, quarrels his elder brother, and calls him the Prince of Coxcombs:

'**Lord Foppington:** Sir, I am proud of being at the head of so prevailing a party.

Young Fashion: Will nothing then provoke thee? Draw, coward!

Lord Foppington: Look you, Tam, your poverty makes your life so burdensome to you, you would provoke me to a quarrel, in hopes to slip through my lungs into my estate, or else to get your self run through the guts to put an end to your pain. But I shall disappoint you in both, *etc.*'

This drolling has too much spirit, the air of it is too free and too handsomely turned for Lord Foppington's character. I grant the Relapser could not afford to lose these sentences. The scene would have suffered by the omission. But then he should have contrived the matter so as that they might have been spoken by Young Fashion in asides, or by some other more proper person.

To go on: Miss Hoyden sparkles too much in conversation. The poet must needs give her a shining line or two, which serves only to make the rest of her dullness the more remarkable. Sir Tunbelly falls into the same misfortune of a wit, and rallies above the force of his capacity: but the place having a mixture of profaneness, I shall forbear to cite it. Now, to what purpose should a fool's coat be embroidered? Finery in the wrong place is but expensive ridiculousness. Besides, I don't perceive the Relapser was in any condition to be thus liberal. And when a poet is not overstocked, to squander away his wit among his blockheads is mere distraction. His men of sense will smart for this prodigality. Loveless, in his discourse of friendship, shall be the first instance. 'Friendship', says he, 'is said to be a plant of tedious growth, its root composed of tender fibres, nice in their taste, *etc.*' By this description the palate of a fibre should be somewhat more nice and distinguishing then the poet's judgement. Let us examine some more of his witty people. Young Fashion fancies, by Miss's forward behaviour, she would have a whole kennel of beaux after her at London. And then, 'Hey to the park, and the play, and the church, and the devil!' Here I conceive the ranging of the period is amiss. For if he had put the play and the devil together, the order of nature and the air of probability had been much better observed.

Afterwards Coupler, being out of breath in coming upstairs to Fashion, asks him, 'Why the ****** [Collier cannot bring himself to quote "plague"] canst thou not lodge upon the ground-floor?' - '**Young Fashion:** Because I love to lie as near heaven as I can.' One would think a spark, just come off his travels, and had made the tour of Italy and France, might have rallied with a better grace! However, if he lodged in a garret, 'tis a good local jest. I had almost forgot one pretty remarkable sentence of Fashion to Lory. 'I shall shew thee,' says he; 'the excess of my passion by being very calm.' Now, since this gentleman was in a vein of talking philosophy to his man, I'm sorry he broke off so quickly. Had he gone on and shown him the excess of a storm and no wind stirring, the topic had been spent and the thought improved to the utmost.

Let us now pass on to Worthy, the Relapser's fine gentleman. This spark sets up for sense and address, and is to have nothing of affectation or conscience to spoil his character. However, to say no more of him, he grows foppish in the last scene, and courts Amanda in fustian and pedantry. First, he gives his periods a turn of versification, and talks prose to her in metre. Now, this is just as agreeable as it would be to ride with one leg and walk with the other. [In Act V, Scene 4, Worthy and Amanda speak partly in blank verse, occasionally degenerating into prose as their emotions rise and fall.] But let him speak for himself. His first business is to bring Amanda to an aversion for her husband; and therefore he persuades her to 'rouse up that spirit women ought to bear, and slight your God if he neglects his angel.' He goes on with his orisons [prayers]: 'With arms of ice receive his cold embraces, and keep your fire for those that come in flames.' Fire and flames is metal upon metal: 'tis false heraldry. 'Extend the arms of mercy to his aid. His zeal may give him title to your pity, although his merit cannot claim your love.' Here you have arms brought in again by head and shoulders. I suppose the design was to keep up the situation of the allegory. But the latter part of the speech is very pithy. He would have her resign her virtue out of civility, and abuse her husband on principles of good nature. Worthy pursues his point, and rises in his address. He falls into a fit of dissection, and hopes to gain his mistress by cutting his throat. He is for ripping up his faithful breast to prove the reality of his passion. Now, when a man courts with his heart in his hand, it must be great cruelty to refuse him! No butcher could have thought of a more moving expedient! However, Amanda continues obstinate, and is not in the usual humour of the stage. Upon this, like a well-bred lover, he seizes her by force and threatens to kill her. 'Nay, struggle not, for all's in vain: or death or victory; I am determined.' In this re-encounter the lady proves too nimble, and slips through his fingers. Upon this disappointment, he cries, 'There's divinity about her, and she has dispensed some portion of it to me.' His passion is metamorphosed in the turn of a hand. He is refined into a platonic admirer, and goes off as like a town spark as you would wish. And so much for the poet's fine gentleman.

I should now examine the Relapser's thoughts and expressions, which are two other things of consideration in the play. The thoughts or sentiments are the expressions of the manners as words are of the thoughts. But the view of the characters has in some measure prevented this enquiry. Leaving this argument, therefore, I shall consider his play with respect to the three unities of time, place, and action [conventions promulgated by Aristotle].

And here the reader may please to take notice, that the design of these rules is to conceal the fiction of the stage, to make the play appear natural, and to give it an air of reality and conversation.

The largest compass for the first unity is twenty-four hours: but a lesser proportion is more regular. To be exact, the time of the history, or fable, should not exceed that of the representation: or in other words, the whole business of the play should not be much longer than the time it takes up in playing.

The second unity is that of place. To observe it, the scene must not wander from one town or country to another. It must continue in the same house, street, or at farthest in the same city, where it was first laid. The reason of this rule depends upon the first. Now, the compass of time being strait [narrow], that of space must bear a correspondent proportion. Long journeys in plays are impracticable. The distances of place must be suited to leisure and possibility; otherwise the supposition will appear unnatural and absurd.

The third unity is that of action. It consists in contriving the chief of business of the play single, and making the concerns of one person distinguishably great above the rest. All the forces of the stage must, as it were, serve under one general; and the lesser intrigues, or underplots, have some relation to the main. The very oppositions must be useful, and appear only to be conquered and counter-mined. To represent two considerable actions independent of each other destroys the beauty of subordination, weakens the contrivance, and dilutes the pleasure. It splits the play, and makes the poem double. He that would see more upon this subject may consult Corneille. To bring this remarks to the case in hand: and here we may observe how the Relapser fails in all the rules above mentioned.

First, his play (by modest computation) takes up a week's work, but five days you must allow it at the lowest. One day must be spent in the first, second, and part of the third act, before Lord Foppington sets forward to Sir Tunbelly. Now the length of the distance, the pomp of the retinue, and the niceness of the person being considered, the journey down and up again cannot be laid under four days. To put this out of doubt, Lord Foppington is particularly careful to tell Coupler how concerned he was not to overdrive, for fear of disordering his coach-horses. The laws of place are no better observed than those of time. In the third act the play is in town, in the fourth act 'tis strolled fifty miles off, and in the fifth act in London again. Here Pegasus stretches it to purpose! This poet is fit to ride a match with witches.

[. . .]

The poet's success in the last unity of action is much the same with the former. Loveless, Amanda, and Berinthia have no share in the main business. These second rate characters are a detached body; their interest is perfectly foreign, and they are neither friends nor enemies to the plot. Young Fashion does not so much as see them till the close of the fifth act, and then they meet only to fill the stage. And yet these persons are in the poet's account very considerable; insomuch that he has misnamed his play from the figure of two of them. This strangeness of persons, distinct company, and inconnexion of affairs destroys the unity of the poem. The contrivance is just as wise as it would be to cut a diamond in two. There is a loss of lustre in the division. Increasing the number abates the value; and by making it more, you make it less.

Thus far I have examined the dramatic merits of the play. And upon enquiry it appears a heap of irregularities. There is neither propriety in the name, nor contrivance in the plot, nor decorum in the characters. 'Tis a thorough contradiction to nature, and impossible in time and place. Its shining graces, as the author calls them, are blasphemy and bawdy, together with a mixture of oaths and cursing. Upon the whole, the Relapser's judgement and his morals are pretty well adjusted. The poet is not much better than the man. As for the profane part, 'tis hideous and superlative: but this I have considered elsewhere. All that I shall observe here is that the author was sensible of this objection. His defence in his preface is most wretched: he pretends to know nothing of the matter, and that 'tis all printed; which only proves his confidence equal to the rest of his virtues. To out-face evidence in this manner is next to the affirming there's no such sin as blasphemy, which is the greatest blasphemy of all. His apology consists in railing at the clergy, a certain sign of ill principles and ill manners. This he does at an unusual rate of rudeness and spite. He calls them the saints with screwed faces and wry mouths. And after a great deal of scurrilous abuse, too gross to be mentioned, he adds:

ATTACK ON VANBRUGH

'If any man happens to be offended at a story of a cock and a bull, and a priest and a bull-dog, I beg his pardon, *etc.*'

This is brave bear-garden language! The Relapser would do well to transport his muse to Samourgan [an academy in Lithuania for the education of bears according to Collier's own note]. There 'tis likely he might find leisure to lick his abortive brat into shape; and meet with proper business for his temper, and encouragement for his talent.

6

Vanbrugh's Vindication

In one sense, Vanbrugh got his retaliation in first. Following the première and immediate success of *The Relapse*, he published the text in December 1696 providing it with a defensive preface, presumably because he was immediately under attack for its "blasphemy and bawdy". The tone of the preface is part sarcastic, part self-deprecatory. Describing his play as "this abortive brat" and "tedious" but not in need of "a long, useless preface", he immediately denies the presence of "blasphemy and bawdy":

> For my part, I cannot find 'em out. If there were any obscene express-
> ions upon the stage, here they are in the print; for I have dealt fairly, I
> have not sunk a syllable that could (though by racking of mysteries) be
> ranged under that head; and yet I believe with a steady faith, there is not
> one woman of a real reputation in town, but when she has read it
> impartially over in her closet, will find it so innocent, she'll think it no
> affront to her prayer book to lay it upon the same shelf.

Writing in 1927, the editor of his complete plays, Bonamy Dobrée, supported his denial of blasphemy but was more ambivalent on the matter of bawdy:

> Indeed, anyone can see that ever to charge blasphemy upon Vanbrugh
> is the sheerest nonsense: it no more entered his head to tilt against reli-
> gion than it did to propagate it: it was one of the things he accepted, and
> he bothered his head about it one way or the other as little as he did about

drinking wine: in neither ought one to be excessive. It is not so easy to clear him from the accusation of bawdy; in fact it must regretfully be admitted that in nearly all his plays Vanbrugh's characters seem clearly to be aware of the physical aspects of love. His constant defence, which may almost be taken as expressing his whole attitude to life, was that in his writing he could not have offended any honest gentlemen of the town, whose friendship or good word is worth the having. He certainly did not avoid treating of the joyous aspects of the flesh, for he knew well enough that a play which had 'No rape, no bawdy, no intrigue, no beau' as he said in the *Prologue* to *Æsop*, did not promise any startling success. And besides, life was life. We may be pretty sure that he did not transgress the bounds acknowledged by the average polite society of his day.

Vanbrugh himself did admit there had been some additional first night bawdiness:

One word more about the bawdy, and I have done. I own the first night this thing was acted some indecencies had like to have happened, but 'twas not my fault. The fine gentleman of the play, drinking his mistress's health in Nantes brandy, from six in the morning to the time he waddled on upon the stage in the evening, had toasted himself up to such a pitch of vigour I confess I once gave Amanda for gone.

The "fine gentleman" in question was the actor George Powell who played Worthy and was a known heavy drinker.

Besides these particular accusations of writing "blasphemy and bawdy", the play seems to have enraged at least one puritan on more general grounds. Even by the time Vanbrugh was writing his preface, word seems to have gone abroad that a cleric was contemplating an attack on the theatre. The playwright had no time (at least in 1696) for such matters:

As for the saints (your thorough-paced ones, I mean, with screwed faces and wry mouths) I despair of them, for they are friends to nobody. They love nothing but their altars and themselves. They have too much zeal to have any charity: they make debauches in piety, as sinners do in wine; and are as quarrelsome in their religion as other people are in their drink; so I hope nobody will mind what they say. But if any man (with flat plod shoes, a little band, greasy hair, and a dirty face, who is wiser than I, at the expense of being forty years older) happens to be offended at a story of a cock and a bull, and a priest and a bulldog, I beg his pardon with all my heart, which I hope I shall obtain by eating my words and making this public recantation.

Tempting though it is to think that Vanbrugh might have predicted Collier's forthcoming onslaught and given us a description of Collier's appearance, it must be remembered that the latter was fourteen and *not* forty years older than Vanbrugh. It is also difficult to imagine Collier spending eighteen months writing his *Short View* - everything about it suggests a greater impetuosity than that.

Before going any further, it is worth noting that for all his excesses Collier wasn't a fool. Bonamy Dobrée is perhaps a little over-generous, but nevertheless provides some useful reminders:

> Not only was Collier a learned man - not, of course, in the front rank of scholars, but widely enough read to be considered learned with respect to general culture - but he was also a good writer ... He was also a clever man, not without cunning, who had felt the pulse of the public and knew exactly what the many-headed monster would greedily swallow. And even today this extravagantly proportioned volume ... is amazing good reading. It is so full of vitality that even where the matter seems fusty and out of date, or the argument quite beside what we have come to think the point, we are hardly tempted to skip. To his own age, inured to the reading of turgid sermons, it must have seemed the sprightliest piece of journalism imaginable.

It must also be noted that, while many of Collier's criticisms and failures to appreciate a joke now strike us as ludicrous, he did make some valid points. Yes, he had a very narrow view of the purpose of drama, as expressed in his opening sentence, and light entertainment seems to have been an alien concept to him. But there are coincidences and implausibilities in *The Relapse* which do not bear much consideration, even if they remain unnoticed in any half-decent production. Collier also fairly draws attention to certain weaknesses in the play's construction: the two plots do go their own separate ways for much of the play's duration. Additionally, the title does imply that Loveless is to be the main character whereas Lord Foppington and Young Fashion's adventures are often the more appealing to an audience. Indeed, it seems that these are the characters who interest Vanbrugh the most.

Given that Vanbrugh was as vigorous in character as Collier, it is not surprising he felt the need to vindicate himself. As Sister Rose Anthony puts it in *The Jeremy Collier Stage Controversy*, "One could scarcely imagine the jaunty captain's not taking up his pen in defence of his attacked plays." Even so, as we have seen, he was by no means the first to answer Collier. He was, however, more successful than some, as J. W. Krutch observes:

He protested that if his plays did not expose vice and folly to ridicule, such had at least been his aim, and he did succeed in proving that while he might be guilty occasionally of considerable freedom in speech and in the full length depiction of rather questionable scenes, he could not fairly be charged with teaching immorality. His illustration of Collier's inability to recognise satire when he sees it and of his unfortunate habit of attributing to the dramatists themselves the opinions of any character is particularly telling. Collier had objected to the following speech of Lord Foppington in *The Relapse*: 'Why faith, madam, Sunday is a vile day, I must confess. A man must have very little to do there that can give an account of the sermon.' Vanbrugh replies very tellingly to the objection by remarking, quite truly, that in the play Lord Foppington does nothing that is not intended to be laughed at and despised.

There was in Restoration Comedy much perversity spoken for the approval of the audience, but this was no example of it, and Collier was so intent on finding matter for objection that he could not recognise satire when he saw it.

What now follows is the principal part of Vanbrugh's self-defence. He is of course answering not only that section of the *Short View* which concentrates on *The Relapse*, but also on Collier's many other charges, for example, Vanbrugh's presentation of Sir Tunbelly Clumsey's chaplain - Bull, relating to his two best known plays. His *A Short Vindication of* The Relapse *and* The Provoked Wife *from Immorality and Profaneness* was published on June 8th, 1698:

When first I saw Mr Collier's performance upon the irregularities of the stage (in which amongst the rest of the gentlemen [playwrights], he's pleased to afford me some particular favours), I was far from designing to trouble either myself or the town with a vindication. I thought his charges against me for immorality and profaneness were grounded upon so much mistake that every one (who had had the curiosity to see the plays, or on this occasion should take the trouble to read them) would easily discover the root of the invective, and that it was the quarrel of his gown, and not of his God, that made him take arms against me.

I found the opinion of my friends and acquaintance the same (at least they told me so) and the righteous as well as the unrighteous persuaded me the attack was so weak, the town would defend itself; that the general's head [Vanbrugh employs an extended military metaphor] was too hot for his conduct to be wise; his shot too much at random ever to make a breach; and that the siege would be raised, without my taking the field.

I easily believed what my laziness made me wish; but I have since found that, by the industry of some people, whose temporal interest engages them in the squabble; and the natural propensity of others, to be fond of anything that is abusive; this lampoon has got credit enough in some places to brand the persons it mentions with almost as bad a character as the author of it has fixed upon himself, by his life and conversation in the world.

I think 'tis therefore now a thing no farther to be laughed at. Should I wholly sit still, those people who are so much mistaken to think I have been busy to encourage immorality, may double their mistake and fancy I profess it. I will therefore endeavour, in a very few pages, to convince the world I have brought nothing upon the stage that proves me more an atheist than a bigot

[. . .]

His play is so wild, I must be content to take the ball as it comes, and return it if I can; which whether I always do or not, however, I believe will prove no great matter, since I hope 'twill appear, where he gives me the rest, he makes but a wide chase: his most threatening strokes end in nothing at all; when he cuts, he's under line; when he forces, he's up in the nets. But to leave tennis and come to the matter.

The first chapter in his book is upon the immodesty of the stage where he tells you how valuable a qualification modesty is in a woman. For my part I am wholly of his mind. I think 'tis almost as valuable in a woman as in a clergyman; and had I the ruling of the roast, the one should neither have a husband, nor the other a benefice without it. If this declaration will not serve to shew I am a friend to it, let us see what proof this gentleman can give of the contrary.

I do not find him over-stocked with quotations in this chapter. He is forced, rather than say nothing, to fall upon poor Miss Hoyden. He does not come to particulars, but only mentions her with others, as an immodest character. What kind of immodesty he means, I can't tell. But I suppose he means lewdness because he generally means wrong. For my part, I know of no bawdy she talks. If the strength of his imagination gives any of her discourse that turn, I suppose it may be owing to the number of bawdy plays he has read which have debauched his taste, and made everything seem salt that comes in his way.

He has but one quotation more in this long chapter, that I'm concerned in. And there he points at *The Provoked Wife*, as if there were something in the 41st page of that play to discountenance modesty in women. But since he did not think fit to acquaint the reader what it was, I will.

Lady Brute and Bellinda [are] speaking of the smuttiness of some plays:

'**Bellinda:** Why does not some reformer or other beat the poet for it?

Lady Brute: Because he is not so sure of our private approbation, as of our public thanks. Well, sure there is not upon earth so impertinent a thing as women's modesty.

Bellinda: Yes, men's fantasque, that obliges us to it. If we quit our modesty, they say we lose our charms; and yet they know that very modesty is affectation, and rail at our hypocrisy.'

Now which way this gentleman will extract anything from hence, to the discouragement of modesty, is beyond my chemistry. 'Tis plainly and directly the contrary. Here are two women (not over virtuous, as their whole character shows), who being alone, and upon the rallying pin, let fall a word between jest and earnest, as if now and then they found themselves cramped by their modesty. But lest this should possibly be mistaken by some part of the audience, less apprehensive of right and wrong than the rest, they are put in mind at the same instant, that (with the men) if they quit their modesty, they lose their charms. Now I thought it was impossible to put the ladies in mind of anything more likely to make them preserve it. I have nothing more laid to my charge in the first chapter.

The second is entitled "The Profaneness of the Stage" which he ranges under two heads: "Their Cursing and Swearing" and "Their Abuse of Religion and the Holy Scriptures". As to swearing, I agree with him in what he says of it in general, that 'tis contrary both to religion and good manners, especially before women; but I say, what he calls swearing in the playhouse (at least where I have to answer for it) is a breach upon neither.

And here I must desire the reader to observe his accusations against me run almost always in general terms. He scarce ever comes to particulars. I hope it will be allowed a good sign on my side, that it always falls to my turn to quote the thing at length in my defence, which he huddles together in my charge. What follows will be an instance of it.

He says in the 57th page (where the business of swearing is upon the tapis [from the French, meaning: under discussion]), with a great deal of honesty and charity, that in this respect *The Relapse* and *The Provoked Wife* are particularly rampant and scandalous.

Would not anybody imagine from hence, that the oaths that were used there, were no less than those of a losing bully at backgammon, or a bilked Hackney coachman? Yet after all, the stretch of the profaneness lies in Lord Foppington's 'Gad', and Miss Hoyden's 'I'Cod'. This is all this gentleman's zeal is in such a ferment about.

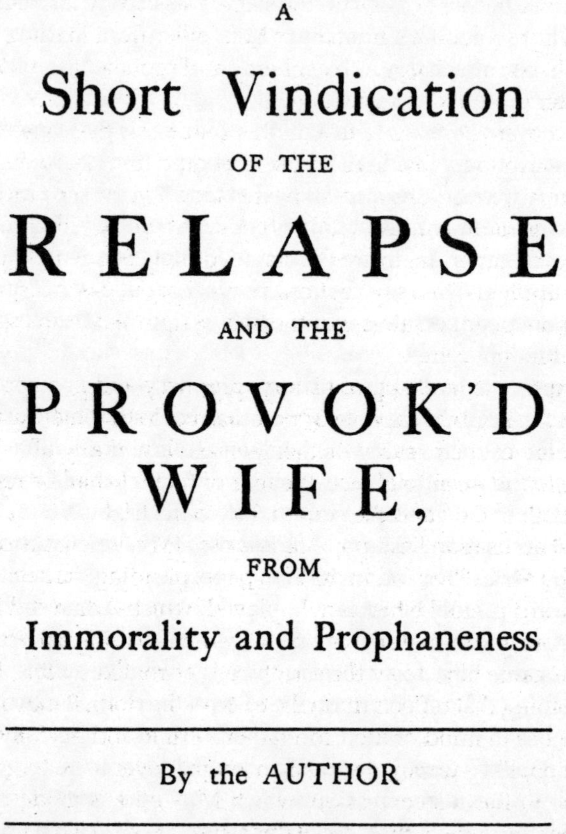

A

Short Vindication

OF THE

RELAPSE

AND THE

PROVOK'D WIFE,

FROM

Immorality and Prophaneness

By the AUTHOR

Figure 4: *A Short Vindication of* The Relapse

Now whether such words are entirely justifiable or not, there is this at least to be said for them; that people of the nicest rank both in their religion and their manners throughout Christendom use them.

In France you meet with 'par Dieu', 'par bleu', 'ma foi' &c., in the constant conversation of the ladies and the clergy, I mean those who are religious even up to bigotry itself; and accordingly we see they are always allowed in their plays: and in England, we meet with an infinity of people (clergy as well as laity) and of the best lives and conversations, who use the words 'I-Gad', 'i-faith', 'codsfish', 'cot's my life' and many more, which all lie liable to the same objection.

Now whether they are right or wrong in doing it, I think at least their example is authority enough for the stage, and should have been enough to have kept so good a Christian as Mr Collier from loading his neighbour with so foul a charge as blasphemy and profaneness, unless he had been better provided to make it good.

The next thing he takes to task in this chapter, is the abuse of religion and holy scripture. Now here I think he should first clearly have proved that no story, phrase, or expression whatsoever in the scripture, whether in the divine, moral or historical part of it, should be either repeated, or so much as alluded to, upon the stage, to how useful an end soever it might be applied. This I say he should have first put past a dispute, before he fell upon me for an abuser of the holy scripture; for unless that be to abuse it, I'm innocent.

The scripture is made up of history, prophecy and precept which are things in their nature capable of no other burlesque than what calls in question either their reality or their sense. Now if any allusion I have made be found even to glance at either of them, I shall be ready to ask pardon both of God and the church. But to the trial.

The first accusation lies upon *The Provoked Wife*, where Rasor is highly blamed by Mr Collier; for, in the 77th page, pleading the same excuse to an untoward prank he had newly played, which Adam did heretofore upon a more unfortunate occasion: that woman having tempted him, the devil overcame him. How the scripture is affronted by this, I can't tell; here's nothing that reflects upon the truth of the story. It may indeed put the audience in mind of their forefather's crime and his folly which, in my opinion, like gunpowder-treason, ought never to be forgot.

The line in Rasor's confession, which Mr Collier's modesty ties him from repeating, makes the close of this sentence: 'And if my prayers were to be heard, her punishment for so doing should be like the serpent's of old, she should lie upon her face all the days of her life.' All I shall say to this, is that an obscene thought must be buried deep indeed, if he does not smell it out; and that I find he has a much greater veneration for the serpent than I have, who shall always make a very great distinction between my respects to God and the Devil.

He runs a muck at all. The next he launches at is my Lord Foppington. And here he is as angry at me for being for religion, as before for being against it (which shows you the man is resolved to quarrel with me). I think his Lordship's words (which he quotes about St James's Church) are beyond all dispute on the minister's side, though not on his congregation's. The indecencies of the place, the levity of the women, and the unseasonable gallantry of the men are exposed in the very lines this gentleman is pleased to quote for their profaneness. For though my Lord Foppington is not supposed to speak what he does to a religious end, yet 'tis so ordered, that his manner of speaking it, together with the character he represents, plainly and obviously instructs the audience (even to the meanest capacity) that what he says of his church-behaviour is designed for their contempt, and not for their imitation. This is so notorious that no school-boy could mistake it. I therefore hope those who observe this man of reformation is capable of giving so good an intention so pernicious a turn, will conclude, when he sat down to write upon the profaneness of the poets, he had nothing less in his head, than to refine the morals of the age.

From the elder brother he falls upon the younger, I suppose because he takes me to be his friend, for I find no other reason for his quarrel. He accuses him for assuring his man Lory, that he has kicked his conscience downstairs and he observes, he says, by the way, that this loose young gentleman is the author's favourite. Now the author observes by the way, that he's always observing wrong; for he has no other proof of his being his favourite than that he has helped him to a wife, who's likely to make his heartache. But I suppose Mr Collier is of opinion that gold can never be bought too dear.

The next flirt is at Worthy and Berinthia; and here he tells you two characters of figure determine the point in defence of pimping. I can pardon his mistake in the business of pimping, because I charitably believe the university may have been the only place he has had any experience of it in, and there 'tis not managed indeed by people of any extraordinary figure. But he may be informed if he pleases, that in this righteous town the profession soars somewhat higher, and that (out of my Lord Mayor's liberties) there are such things as Worthy and Berinthia to be found. I brought them upon the stage to show the world how much the trade was improved; but this gentleman I find won't take my word for it.

Nurse is to have the next kick of the breech, and 'tis for being too profane. But that's left for me to quote again: for his part, all he repeats from her is that 'his worship (Young Fashion) overflows with his mercy and his bounty. He is not only pleased to forgive us our sins but which is more than all, has prevailed with me to become the wife of thy bosom.'

This he says is dull: why so 'tis and so is he, for thinking it worth his finding fault with, unless it had been spoke by somebody else than a nurse, and to somebody else than Mr Bull. But the profane stuff he says precedes it, I'll acquaint the reader with. She says (speaking to the chaplain)

'Roger, are not you a wicked man, Roger, to set your strength against a weak woman, and persuade her it was no sin to conceal miss's nuptials? My conscience flies in my face for it, thou priest of Baal and I find by woeful experience, thy absolution is not worth an old cassock.'

The reader may here be pleased to take notice what this gentleman would consider profaneness, if he were once in the saddle with a good pair of spurs upon his heels. I have all manner of respect for the clergy but I should be very sorry to see the day that a nurse's cracking a jest upon a chaplain (where it has no allusion to religion) should be brought within the verge of profaneness. But the next chapter, about the abuse of the clergy, will give occasion for some more remarks of this kind.

Amanda comes next, I thought she might have escaped but it seems, with all her virtue, she charges the Bible with untruths, and says:

'Good Gods, what slippery stuff are men composed of! Sure the account of their creation's false and 'twas the woman's rib that they were formed of.'

I'm sorry the gentleman who wrote this speech of Amanda's is not here to defend himself but he being gone away with the Czar, who has made him Poet Laureate of Muscovy, I can do no less for the favour he intended me, than to say this in his justification. That to my knowledge he has too much veneration for the Bible, to intend this a charge upon the truth of it and that it appears very plain to me, Amanda intended no more to call it in question by those words, than Mr Collier's wife might be supposed to do, if from some observations upon his book, she should say, 'Sure 'tis a mistake in the New Testament that the fruits of the Spirit are modesty, temperance, justice, meekness, charity, *etc.*; for my Jeremy is a spiritual person, yet has not one of these marks about him.'

Worthy follows. And I am threatened with no less than eternal damnàtion, for making him say to his procuress (when she had promised to do what he'd have her) 'Thou Angel of Light, let me fall down and adore thee.' But I am not commended for the answer she makes him, to put the audience in mind, she was not supposed to deserve that compliment, 'Thou Minister of Darkness get up again, for I hate to see the Devil at his devotions.' If Mr Collier had quoted this too, he had given a better character of me and I think of himself.

Vanbrugh next answers some of Collier's charges against *The Provoked Wife* before returning to his defence of *The Relapse*:

Young Fashion is next accused for saying to Lory (when he had a prospect of getting Miss Hoyden) 'Providence, thou seest at last, takes care of men of merit.' This surely is a very poor charge and a critic must be reduced to short commons to chop at it. Everybody knows the word 'providence' in common discourse goes for fortune. If it be answered, let it go for what it will, it is in strictness God Almighty; I answer again, that if you go to strictness, fortune is God Almighty as much as providence, and yet no one ever thought it blasphemy to say 'fortune's blind' or 'fortune favours fools'. And the reason why it is not thought so, is because 'tis known it is not meant so.

Berinthia comes again, and is blamed for telling Amanda that Worthy had taken her to pieces like a text and preached upon every part of her. This is called a lewd and profane allegory. I confess it has, at a glance, the appearance of somewhat which it is not, and that, methinks, Mr Collier might have been content to have charged it with. But he always takes care to stretch that way that becomes him least, and so is sure to be in the wrong himself, whether I am so or not.

Neither the woman in general, nor any particular part about her, is likened to the text. The simile lies between the manner of a minister's using his text and Worthy's flourishing upon his mistress. So that the profanation's got in the wrong place here again. But supposing the minister to be as Mr Collier would have him, as sacred a thing as his text, there's nothing here that burlesques him. 'Tis a simile indeed, but a very inoffensive one, for it abuses nobody, and as to the lewdness of it, I refer myself to the reader here again, whether this gentleman does not give us another instance of his having a very quick nose, when some certain things are in the wind. I believe, had the obscenity he has rooted up here, been buried as deep in his churchyard, the yarest boar in his parish would hardly have tossed up his snout at it.

Berinthia's close of her speech, 'Now consider of what has been said, and heaven give you grace to put it in practice', brings up the rear of the attack in this chapter. This I own are words often used at the close of a sermon, and therefore perhaps might as well have been let alone here. A known pulpit-expression sounds loose upon the stage, though nothing is really affronted by it; for that I think in this case is very plain, to anybody that considers, who it is that speaks these words, and her manner of doing it. There's nothing serious in it, as if she would persuade either Amanda or the audience that heaven approved what she was doing. 'Tis only a loose expression, suitable to the character she represents, which, throughout the play, sufficiently shows, she's brought upon the stage to ridicule something that's off on it.

These three or four last quotations Mr Collier says are downright blasphemy, and within the law. I hope the reader will perceive he says wrong.

The next chapter is upon the abuse of the clergy and here we are come to the spring of the quarrel. I believe whoever reads Mr Collier need take very little pains to find out that, in all probability, had the poets never discovered a rent in the gown, he had done by religion, as I do by my brethren, left it to shift for it self.

In starting this point, he opens a large field for an adversary to rove in: he unbars the gate of the town, forgetting the weakness of the garrison. Were I the Governor or not, I'd commend him for his courage, much more than for his prudence.

I once thought to have said a great deal upon this occasion but I have changed my mind, and will trouble the reader with no more than I think is necessary to clear myself from the charge of ridiculing the function of a clergyman.

I'm as fully convinced, as the most pious divine, or the most refined politician can wish me, how necessary the practice of all moral virtues is to our happiness in this world, as well as to that of another. And this opinion has its natural consequence with me, which is to give me a regard to every instrument of their promotion.

The institution of the clergy I own to be both in the intention and capacity the most effectual of all; I have therefore for the function all imaginable deference, and would do all things to support it in such a kind of credit as will render it most formidable in the execution of its design. But in this Mr Collier and I, I doubt, are not like to agree.

He is of opinion, that riches and plenty, title, state and dominion, give a majesty to precept, and cry 'Place' [make room] for it wherever it comes; that Christ and his Apostles took the thing by the wrong handle; and that the Pope and his Cardinals have much refined upon them in the policy of instruction. That should a vicar, like St John, feed on locusts and wild honey, his parish would think he had too ill a taste for himself to cater for them; and that a Bishop who, like St Paul, should decline temporal dominion, would shew himself such an ass, his advice would go for nothing.

This I find is Mr Collier's opinion; and if ever I take orders, I will not swear it shall not be mine. But then I fear I shall continue in my heresy; three articles of which are these: 1) That the Shepherd, who has least business at home in his house, is likely to take the most care of his flock. 2) That he who finds fault with the sauce he greedily sops his bread in, gives very good cause to suspect he'd fain keep it all to himself. 3) That he who is strict in the performance of his duty, needs no other help, to be respected in his office.

[. . .]

In *The Relapse*, Mr Collier complains that his brother Bull wishes the married couple joy in language so horribly smutty and profane, to transcribe it would blot the paper too much. I am therefore put upon the old necessity to transcribe it for him, that the world may see what this honest gentleman would pass upon them as well as me, for profane, had he as long a sword in his hand as the Pope has in his.

Bull's words are these:

'I most humbly thank your honours; and I hope, since it has been my lot to join you in the holy hands of wedlock, you will so well cultivate the soil, which I have craved a blessing on, that your children may swarm about you like bees about a honey-comb.'

These are the words he calls horribly smutty and profane.

The next quarrel's about I don't know what; nor can light of anybody that can tell me. He says, 'Young Fashion's desiring Mr Bull to make haste to Sir Tunbelly; he answers him very decently, "I fly, my good Lord."' What this gentleman means by this quotation, I can't imagine; but I can answer for the other gentleman, he only meant he'd make haste.

He quotes two or three sentences more of Bull's which are just as profane as the rest. He concludes, that the chaplain has a great deal of heavy stuff upon his hands and his chief quarrel to me here is, that I have not made him a wit. I ask pardon, that I could suppose a Deputy-Lieutenant's chaplain could be a blockhead but I thought, if there was such a thing, he was as likely to be met with in Sir Tunbelly's house, as anywhere. If ever I write the character of a gentleman where a chaplain like Mr Collier is to have the direction of the family, I'll endeavour to give him more sense, that I may qualify him for more mischief.

[. . .]

Thus violently does his zeal to the priesthood run away with him. Some clergyman, methinks, should help to stop him; and I almost persuade myself there will. There is still in the gown of the Church of England a very great number of men, both learned, wise, and good, who thoroughly understand religion, and truly love it. From amongst these I flatter myself some hero will start up, and with the naked virtue of an old generous Roman, appear a patriot for religion indeed; with a trumpet before him proclaim the secrets of the cloister, and by discovering the disease, guide the world to the cure of it.

Vanbrugh continues in this vein, eulogising the Church of England and criticising the Church of Rome.

The next chapter is upon the encouragement of immorality by the stage; and here Constant [in *The Provoked Wife*] is fallen upon, for pretending to be a fine gentleman, without living up to the exact rules of religion. If Mr Collier excludes everyone from that character that does not, I doubt he'll have a more general quarrel to make up with the gentlemen of England, than I have with the Lords, though he tells them I have highly affronted them. But I would fain know after all, upon what foundation he lays so positive a position, that Constant is my model for a fine gentleman and that he is brought upon the stage for imitation.

He might as well say, if I brought his character upon the stage, I designed it a model to the clergy and yet I believe most people would take it the other way. O, but these kind of fine gentlemen, he says, are always prosperous in their undertakings, and their vice under no kind of detection; for in the Fifth Act of the play, they are usually rewarded with a wife or a mistress. And suppose I should reward him with a bishopric in the Fifth Act, would that mend his character? I have too great a veneration for the clergy, to believe that would make 'em follow his steps. And yet (with all due respect to the ladies) take one amour with another, the bishopric may prove as weighty a reward as a wife or a mistress either. He says, 'Mr Bull was abused upon the stage', yet he got a wife and a benefice too. Poor Constant has neither, nay, he has not got even his mistress yet, he had not, at least, when the play was last acted. But this honest doctor, I find, does not yet understand the nature of comedy, though he has made it his study so long. For the business of comedy is to shew people what they should do, by representing them upon the stage, doing what they should not. Nor is there any necessity a philosopher should stand by, like an interpreter at a poppet-show, to explain the moral to the audience. The mystery is seldom so deep, but the pit and boxes can dive into it and 'tis their example out of the playhouse, that chiefly influences the galleries. The stage is a glass for the world to view itself in. People ought therefore to see themselves as they are; if it makes their faces too fair, they won't know they are dirty, and by consequence will neglect to wash 'em.

Vanbrugh then discusses various points relating to *The Provoked Wife* before turning his attention to the section of the *Short View* relating specifically to *The Relapse*.

I am now come to thank the gentleman for the last of his favours in which he is so generous to bestow a chapter entire upon me. I'm extremely obliged to him for it, since 'tis more than ever he promised me, for in the title of his book, he designs to correct the stage only for the immorality and profaneness of it. And indeed I think that was all his business with it. But he has since considered better of the matter, and rather than quit his hold, falls a criticising upon plots, characters, words, dialogue, &c., even to telling us when our fine gentlemen make love in the prevailing strain, and when not. This gives us a farther view of his studies; but, I think, if he kept to his text, he had given us a better view of a clergyman.

It may, perhaps, be expected I should say more in answer to this chapter, than to all that has gone before it; the sense of the play being attacked here, much more than the moral, which those who will take Mr Collier's word for my principles, must believe I am least concerned for. But I shall satisfy 'em of the contrary, by leaving the sense to answer for itself if it can. I'll only say this for it in general: that it looks as if a play were not overloaded with blunders, when so painstaking a corrector is reduced to the wretched necessity of spending his satire upon 'fire' and 'flames', being in the same line; and 'arms' twice in the same speech, though at six lines distance one from the other. This looks as if the critic were rather duller than the poet. But when men fight in a passion, 'tis usual to make insignificant thrusts; most of his are so wide, they need no parrying and those that hit, are so weak, they make no wound.

I don't pretend, however, to have observed the nicety of the rule in this play. I write it in as much haste (though not in so much fury) as he has done his remarks upon it. 'Tis therefore possible I may have made as many foolish mistakes.

I could however say a great deal against the too exact observance of what's called the rules of the stage, and the crowding a comedy with a great deal of intricate plot. I believe I could shew, that the chief entertainment, as well as the moral, lies much more in the characters and the dialogue, than in the business and the event. And I can assure Mr Collier, if I would have weakened the diversion, I could have avoided all his objections, and have been at the expense of much less pains than I have. And this is all the answer I shall make to 'em, except what tumbles in my way, as I'm observing the foul play he shows me, in setting *The Relapse* in so wrong a light as he does, at his opening of the fable on it.

In the first page of his remarks upon this play, he says I have given it a wrong title, *The Relapse::* or *Virtue in Danger*, relating only to Loveless and Amanda, who are characters of an inferior consideration and that 'The Younger Brother' or 'The Fortunate Cheat', had been much more proper, because Young Fashion is, without competition, the principal person in the comedy.

In reading this gentleman's book, I have been often at loss to know when he's playing the knave, and when he's playing the fool, nor can I decide which he's at now. But this I'm sure, Young Fashion is no more the principal person of the play, than he's the best character in the church, nor has he any reason to suppose him so, but because he brings up the rear of the most insignificant part of the play, and happens to be the bridegroom in the close of it.

I won't say anything here irreverently of matrimony, because *à la Françoise* bigotry runs high, and by all I see, we are in a fair way to make a sacrament of it again. But this I may say, that I had full as much respect for Young Fashion, while he was a bachelor, and yet I think while he was so, Loveless has a part, that from people who desire to be the better for plays, might draw a little more attention. In short, my Lord Foppington, and the bridegroom, and the bride, and the Justice, and the matchmaker, and the nurse, and the parson at the rear of 'em, are the inferior persons of the play (I mean as to their business), and what they do, is more to divert the audience, by something particular and whimsical in their humours, than to instruct 'em in anything that may be drawn from their morals, though several useful things may in passing be picked up from 'em too.

This is as distinct from the main intention of the play, as the business of Gomez is the Spanish friar. I shan't here enter into the contest, whether it be right to have two distinct designs in one play. I'll only say, I think when there are so, if they are both entertaining, then 'tis right; if they are not, 'tis wrong. But the dispute here is, where lies the principal business in *The Relapse*? Mr Collier decides it roundly for the wedding-house, because there's best cheer; his patron, Sir Tunbelly, has got a good venison-pasty for him, and such a tankard of ale, as has made him quite forget the moral reflections he should have made upon the disorders that are slipped into Loveless's house, by his being too positive in his own strength, and forgetting that 'Lead us not into Temptation', is a petition in our prayers, which was thought fit to be tacked to that for our daily bread.

And here my design was such, I little thought it would ever have been ridiculed by a clergyman. 'Twas in a few words this.

I observed in a play, called *Love's Last Shift: or The Fool in Fashion*, a debauchee pay so dear for his lewdness, and his folly, as from a plentiful fortune, and a creditable establishment in the world, so be reduced by his extravagance to want even the common supports of life. In this distress, providence (I ask Mr Collier's pardon for using the word) by an unexpected turn in his favour, restores him to peace and plenty. And there is that in the manner of doing it, and the instrument that brings it to pass, as must necessarily give him the most sensible view, both of his misery past, from the looseness of his life, and his happiness to come, in the reform of it. In the close of the play, he's left thoroughly convinced it must therefore be done, and as fully determined to do it.

For my part, I thought him so indisputably in the right; and he appeared to me to be got into so agreeable a tract of life, that I often took a pleasure to indulge a musing fancy, and suppose myself in his place. The happiness I saw him possessed of, I looked upon as a jewel of a very great worth, which naturally lead me to the fear of losing it; I therefore considered by what enemies 'twas most likely to be attacked, and that directed me in the plan of the works that were most probable to defend it. I saw but one danger in solitude and retirement, and I saw a thousand in the bustle of the world; I therefore in a moment determined for the contrary, and supposed Loveless and Amanda gone out of town.

I found these reflections of some service to myself, and so (being drawn into the folly of writing a play) I resolved the town should share them with me. But it seems they are so little to Mr Collier's taste, he'll neither eat the meat himself, nor say grace to it for anybody else. I'll try however if the following account will recommend it to him.

Loveless and his wife appear in the start of the play, happy in their retirement and, in all human prospect, likely to continue so - if they continue where they are. As for Amanda, she's so pleased with her solitude, she desires never to leave it; and the adventures that happen upon her being forced to it, may caution a husband (if he pleases) against being so very importunate to bring his wife (how virtuous soever) into the way of mischief, when she herself is content to keep out of it.

Loveless is so thoroughly weaned from the taste of his debauches, he has not a thought toward the stage where they used to be acted. 'Tis business, not pleasure, brings him thither again, and his wife can't persuade him there's the least danger of a relapse; he's proud to think on what a rock his reformation is built, and resolves she herself shall be a witness, that though the winds blow and the billows roar, yet nothing can prevail against it.

To town in short they come, and temptation's set at defiance. 'Lead us not into' it is a request he has no farther occasion for. The first place he tries his strength is where he used to be the most sensible of his weakness.

He could resist no woman heretofore; he'll now show he can stand a battalion of them; so to the playhouse he goes, and with a smile of contempt looks coolly into the boxes. But Berinthia is there to chastise his presumption: he discovers her beauty, but despises her charms; and is fond of himself that so unmoved he can consider them. He finds a pleasure indeed in viewing the curiosity, but 'tis only to contemplate the skill of the contriver. As for desire, he's satisfied he has none; let the symptoms be what they will, he's free from the disease. He may gaze upon the lady till he grows a statue in the place, but he's sure he's in love with none but his wife. Home he comes, and gives her an account of what he has seen; she's alarmed at the story, and looks back to her retirement. He blames her suspicion, and all is silent again. When fate (here's blasphemy again) so disposes things, that the temptation's brought home to his door and his wife has the misfortune to invite it into her house. In short; Berinthia becomes one of the family. She's beautiful in her person, gay in her temper, coquet in her behaviour, and warm in her desires. In a word, the battery is so near, there's no standing the shot, constancy's beaten down; the breach is made, resolution gives ground, and the town's taken.

This I designed for a natural instance of the frailty of mankind, even in his most fixed determinations; and for a mark upon the defect of the most steady resolve, without that necessary guard, of keeping out of temptation. But I had still a farther end in Loveless's relapse, and indeed much the same with that in *The Provoked Wife*, though in different kind of characters; these latter being a little more refined, which places the moral in a more reasonable, and I think, a more agreeable view. There the provocation is from Brute, and by consequence cannot be supposed to sting a woman so much, as if it had come from a more reasonable creature. The lady therefore that gives herself a loose upon it [indulges or embraces such provocation], could not naturally be represented the best of her sex. Virtuous (upon some ground or other) there was a necessity of making her; but it appears by a strain of levity that runs through her discourse, she owed it more to form, or apprehension, or at best to some few notions of gratitude to her husband, for taking her with an inferior fortune, than to any principle of religion, or an extraordinary modesty. 'Twas therefore not extremely to be wondered at, that when her husband made her house uneasy for her at home, she should be prevailed with to accept some diversions abroad. However, since she was regular while he was kind, the fable may be a useful admonition to men who have wives, and would keep them to themselves, not to build their security so entirely upon their ladies' principles, as to venture to pull from under her all the political props of her virtue.

But in the adventures of Loveless and Amanda, the caution is carried farther. Here's a woman whose virtue is raised upon the utmost strength of foundation: religion, modesty and love, defend it. It looks so sacred one would think no mortal durst approach it; and seems so fixed one would believe no engine could shake it: yet loosen one stone, the weather works in, and the structure moulders apace to decay. She discovers her husband's return to his inconstancy. The unsteadiness of his love gives her a contempt of his person; and what lessens her opinion, declines her inclination. As her passion for him is abated, that against him is inflamed; and as her anger increases, her reason's confused. Her judgement in disorder, her religion's unhinged; and that fence being broken, she lies widely exposed. Worthy's too sensible of the advantage to let slip the occasion: he has intelligence of the vacancy, and puts in for the place.

Poor Amanda's persuaded he's only to be her friend, and that all he asks is to be admitted as a comforter in her afflictions. But when people are sick, they are so fond of a cordial that when they get it to their nose, they are apt to take too much of it.

She finds in his company such a relief to her pain she desires the physician may be always in her sight. She grows pleased with his person as well as his advice, yet she's sure he can never put her virtue in danger. But she might have remembered her husband was once of the same opinion; and have taken warning from him, as the audience, I intended, should do from them both.

This was the design of the play; which I think is something of so much greater importance than Young Fashion's marrying Miss Hoyden, that if I had called it 'The Younger Brother', or 'The Fortunate Cheat', instead of *The Relapse:* or *Virtue in Danger*, I had been just as much in the wrong, as Mr Collier is now.

His reason, I remember, why Loveless can't be reckoned a principal part is because he sinks in the fourth act. But I can tell him, if the play had sunk in the fourth act too, it had been better than 'tis, by just twenty per cent. However, though Loveless's affair is brought about in the fourth act, Amanda's last adventure is towards the end of the fifth. But this is only a cavil from the formality of the critics - which is always well broken into, if the diversion's increased by it, and nature not turned top-side-turvy. If therefore nothing but the critics (I mean such as Mr Collier) find themselves shocked by the disorders of this play, I think I need trouble myself as little to justify what's past as I own I should to mend it, in anything to come; had I thoughts of meddling any more with the stage. But to draw to an end.

I have reserved for the close of this paper, one observation (a home one I think) upon the unfair dealing of this reverend gentleman; which shows at once the rancour of his venom, the stretch of his injustice, and by a moral consequence, I think, the extremity of his folly: for sure there cannot be a greater than for a man of his coat, at the very instant he's declaiming against the crimes of the age, to lay himself so open, to be hit in the most immoral blot of life, which that of slander undisputedly is.

To explain. I beg the reader will bestow one moment's reflection upon the pains he has taken to make Young Fashion and his affair pass for the principal concern of the comedy; which he only has done in hopes to sink the useful moral of the play, which he knew lay in the other part of it and would unavoidably have appeared in judgement against his reflections upon the whole - if he had not taken this way to stifle the evidence. He therefore carries on the imposture to that degree, as at last to slubber over the conclusive scene between Worthy and Amanda, as if there were no meaning of importance in it. Nay, his rage is so great (to find the stamp of immorality he would fain have fixed upon this play, so cleanly washed off by the close of this scene) that he cares not what folly he commits; and therefore in his heats (rather than commend it for the alarm it gives to lewdness by Worthy's reflections upon Amanda's refusal) he turns him into ridicule for an insipid Platonic; by which we may guess, had he been in the fine gentleman's place, the lady would not have escaped as she did. I'll repeat Worthy's words, with the doctor's use of them, and so have done.

'**Worthy:** Sure there's divinity about her, and she has dispensed some portion of it to me. For what but now was the wild flame of love, or (to dissect that specious term) the vile, the gross desires of flesh and blood, is in a moment turned to adoration. The coarser appetite of nature's gone, and 'tis methinks the food of angels I require. How long this influence may last, heaven knows; but in this moment of my purity, I could on her own terms accept her heart. Yes, lovely woman, I can accept it, for now 'tis doubly worth my care. Your charms are much increased since this adorned. When truth's extorted from us, then we own the robe of virtue is a graceful habit.

> Could women but our secret councils scan,
> Could they but reach the deep reserves of man;
> They'd wear it on, that that of love might last:
> For when they throw off one, we soon the other cast.
> Their sympathy is such -
> The fate of one, the other scarce can fly,
> They live together, and together dye.'

This reflection Worthy makes to himself, upon Amanda's having virtue enough to resist him, when he plainly saw she lay under a pressing temptation.

Now when 'tis considered, that upon the stage the person who speaks in a soliloquy is always supposed to deliver his real thoughts to the audience, I think it must be granted there never was a home check given to the lewdness of women in any play whatsoever. For what in nature can touch them nearer than to see a man, after all the pains he has taken and the eager arguments he has used, lay open his heart, and frankly confess, had he gained his mistress, she had lost her gallant.

This I thought was a turn so little suited to comedy, that I confess I was afraid the rigour of the moral would have damned the play. But it seems everybody could relish it but a clergyman. Mr Collier's words are these:

'Amanda continues obstinate, and is not in the usual humour of the stage: upon this, like a well-bred lover he seizes her by force, and threatens to kill her. (By the way, this purblind divine might have seen 'twas himself, not his mistress, he threatened.) In this rencounter the lady proves too nimble, and slips through his fingers. Upon this disappointment he cries, 'There's divinity about her, and she has dispensed some portion of it to me.' His passion is metamorphosed in the turn of a hand. He's refined into a Platonic admirer, and goes off as like a town-spark as you would wish. And so much for the poet's fine gentleman.'

The world may see by this, what a contempt the doctor has for a spark that can make no better use of his mistress than to admire her for her virtue. This, methinks, is something so very extraordinary in a clergyman that I almost fancy when he and I are fast asleep in our graves, those who shall read what we both have produced, will be apt to conclude there's a mistake in the tradition about the authors; and that 'twas the reforming divine writ the play, and the scandalous poet the remarks upon it.

7

The Playwrights Reply

The debate continued throughout that summer. Following Vanbrugh's *Vindication* of himself and his plays, a succession of pamphlets, accusations and counter-accusations were published by London booksellers. Many, especially those published anonymously, now seem both tedious and verbose as critics attacked and counter-attacked each other. In this chapter, we shall consider the more telling and especially the responses of the playwrights themselves.

Towards the end of June, the anonymous, and garrulous, author of *A Defence of Dramatic Poetry* published *A Farther Defence*, notable more for its mockery of Collier than for any quality of argument:

'Tis yet a little more strange that this author [Collier] should quarrel with the stage for this boldness with the clergy when he himself has furnished it with one of the most divertive characters for a comedy . . . His very remarks upon *The Relapse* . . . would supply a subject for a whole farce.

He also implies that, although "religion and reformation was the pretence" of Collier's attack, he was actually inspired by "fifty guineas copy-money". Another digression in this *Farther Defence* corrects the gossip of the time:

It goes for current authority round the whole town that Mr Dryden himself had publicly declared it [the *Short View*] unanswerable and had thanked Mr Collier for the just correction he had given him; and that Mr Congreve and some other great authors had made much the same declaration - which is all so notoriously false, so egregious a lie, that Mr Dryden particularly looked upon it as a pile of malice, ill-nature and uncharitableness.

As was noted in Chapter Four, Dryden had already reacted to Collier's outburst and would do so again - in most cases accepting, at least in part, Collier's strictures [*pace* the author of the *Farther Defence*]. Of the other four playwrights singled out for special attack by Collier, D'Urfey and Congreve entered the debate during July 1698. Wycherley, so far as we can tell, gave no direct reply, although yet another anonymous publication *A Vindication of the Stage* has been ascribed to him but this is disputed. The sixth of Collier's would-be victims, Otway, had died in 1685.

Thomas D'Urfey had been born Tom Durfey in 1653 and was regularly described as "a scurrilous fellow" but was also a friend of both Charles II and James II. He wrote much, including songs, satires, melodramas and farces - and the 27-page preface to his comedy *The Campaigners*. This is not so much an answer to Collier's criticisms (of, for example, neglecting the dramatic unities) as an angry, peevish attack on the cleric:

> But let state revolvers
> And treason absolvers
> Excuse if I say:
> The scoundrel that chooses
> To cry down the muses
> Would cry down the King.

From 1698 on, D'Urfey was frequently prosecuted for profanity. Indeed, in the months that followed, several actors were also prosecuted for taking the name of God in vain, and verdicts obtained against them. In 1701, Vanbrugh's *The Provoked Wife* was similarly condemned. Even so, there was no sudden disappearance of blasphemy from the stage. Three days after the appearance of D'Urfey's *Preface* in print, on July 12, 1698, Congreve published his much more substantial vindication. Running to 119 pages, its comparably lengthy title is *Amendments of Mr Collier's False and Imperfect Citations etc., from* The Old Bachelor, The Double Dealer, Love for Love, The Mourning Bride. *By the Author of Those Plays.*

William Congreve was born in 1670 at Bardsey, near Leeds, in Yorkshire. His father was a younger son of an old Staffordshire family, and fought for the King during the Civil War. After the Restoration, the family settled in Ireland where Congreve went to school, and then to university at Dublin where he was a contemporary of Swift. He then went to London to study law - only to give it up in order to write for the stage. When *The Old Bachelor* was produced in 1693, he was hailed by "the gentry, the pits and Dryden" as "a rising star". *The Double Dealer* appeared in 1694 but became popular only when commended by Queen Mary. Congreve had a more immediate success with *Love for Love* the following year. These three comedies were followed by his sole tragedy, *The Mourning Bride* (1697) - a play chiefly remembered for its lines "Music hath charms to soothe a savage breast" and

Heaven has no rage like love to hatred turned,

Nor hell a fury like a woman scorned.

Professor Krutch describes his comedies as "cynical pictures of contemporary society ... unconcerned with any moral consideration". Allardyce Nicholl suggests the same: "There is no puritanical streak, as in the later Wycherley." But if we consider *Love for Love*, we discover that the rake-hero, Valentine, professes libertinism but does not practise it. He has illegitimate children, but his decision to marry excuses him in Congreve's and the audience's eyes. Congreve defends his creation: "In short, the character is a mixed character; his faults are fewer than his good qualities." Not enough, of course, for Collier.

It was, however, *The Double Dealer* which, among Congreve's works, attracted most condemnation: "There are but four ladies in this play and three of the biggest of them are whores." Collier also damned it for blasphemy, a coachman is called Jehu, irreverent treatment of the clergy, in the person of the chaplain Saygrace, and for various profanities and obscenities.

It has to be admitted that Congreve's self-defence is not as witty as might have been expected. He begins his *Amendments* by admitting that he is replying to Collier only because he might otherwise have been thought idle or lazy:

I have no intention to examine all the absurdities and falsehoods in Mr Collier's book.

Nor is his reply going to answer Collier's main argument:

> Least of all would I undertake to defend the corruptions of the stage ...
> I will not justify any of my own errors; I am sensible of many . . . My
> intention is to do little else but to restore those passages to their primi-
> tive station, which have suffered so much in being transplanted by him:
> I will remove them from his dung hill and replant them in the field of
> nature; and when I have washed them of that filth which they have
> contracted in passing through his very dirty hands, let their own inno-
> cence protect them.

Or, as he suggests a little later, Collier has "blackened the characters
with his own smut".

Congreve goes on to lay down four propositions. In the first, he says
he will consider Collier's criticisms in the light of Aristotle's *Definition
of Comedy*. Congreve says that, in accordance with that definition, we
are to consider comedy as the "imitation" of the "worst" class of people
- worst not in 'quality' but in manners:

> For men are to be laughed out of their vices in comedy: the business of
> comedy is to delight, as well as to instruct. And as vicious people are
> made ashamed of their follies or faults by seeing them exposed in a
> ridiculous manner, so are good people at once both warned and diverted
> at their expense.

With his second proposition, Congreve states that writers of comedy must create "foolish" characters but that this does not mean that
they (the playwrights) are consequently foolish or corrupt:

> It were very hard that a painter should be believed to resemble all the
> ugly faces he draws.

His third proposition states that Collier frequently takes remarks
out of context and then passes invalid judgements, while his fourth is
concerned with Collier's chapter on the profaneness of the English
stage (the second chapter of the *Short View*). Not only does Congreve
firmly disagree with Collier but states with some emphasis that:

> ... when words are applied to sacred things, and with a purpose to treat
> of sacred things, they ought to be understood accordingly; but when they
> are otherwise applied, the diversity of the subject gives a diversity of
> signifaction.

With his terms defined, Congreve then sets about refuting Collier's
charges of immodesty, profaneness and immorality - but seems happy

to ignore the charge of abusing the clergy. Indeed, he often digresses to pick tiny holes in Collier's argument:

> He is very merry . . . in laughing at 'wasting air' . . . But where does he meet with 'wasting air'? Not in *The Mourning Bride*; for in that play it is printed 'wafting air'.

While Congreve does make a proper plea for the theatre being regarded as a necessary diversion or entertainment (echoes here of Dennis's *Usefulness of the Stage*), he is more often content merely to accuse Collier of prejudice and scurrility. Indeed, many commentators have suggested that Congreve's real answer to Collier was *The Way of the World* (1700) in which Congreve warns his audience in the *Prologue*:

> Satire, he thinks, you ought not to expect;
> For so reformed a town, who dares to correct?

In the same play, Lady Wishfort sarcastically tells Mrs Marwood, "There are some books over the chimney - the *Short View of the Stage*, with Bunyan's works to entertain you." *The Way of the World* had only moderate success and it is said that, because of that and because of Collier's attacks upon him, Congreve gave up writing for the stage - aged 30. As one biographer, J. C. Hodges in *William Congreve the Man* (New York 1941), has put it, he would no longer "prostitute his muse to the lower taste of the town" since "the London audience would not accept the type of high comedy that now satisfied his artistic taste".

In many ways, Congreve's response to Collier is disappointing: it lacks the wit that illuminates his plays - nor is it tightly argued. For example, as Professor Krutch has pointed out:

> Congreve is right as long as he maintains that there is no reason why he should not ridicule a foolish clergyman, but he is insincere and unwise when he maintains that he did not intend ridicule when he christened one 'Mr Prig' . . . On the whole, Congreve's reply is hastily written and not very successful. He showed that Collier sometimes exaggerated, but he made no very satisfactory reply to the principal charge, i.e. that he represented vice in an attractive light and made vicious characters successful.

Meanwhile, his *Amendments* had provoked various reactions. September of that year saw the publication of four anonymous works. Two of them commended Collier and attacked Congreve, while a third, possibly by a journalist called George Ridpath, also supported Collier. Under the title *The Stage Condemned*, this 216-page book moved the debate back to a political level, equated the theatre with Popery and requested all English ladies and gentlewomen to absent themselves from the playhouse. The fourth of the September publications, *The Immorality of the English Pulpit*, took a very different standpoint. Specifically attacking the third chapter of the *Short View* (the abuse of clergy), it is full of acid and venom. This anonymous author also makes the valid point that it was under the Stuarts, whom Collier had supported, that the stage had developed in the way it had.

In November, Collier felt impelled to return to the attack - or rather *A Defence of the Short View*:

> Since the publishing my late *View*, I have been plentifully railed on in print . . . but being charged with miscitations and unfair dealing, 'twas requisite to say something.

"Something" in this case meant 139 pages!

Having been regularly attacked for his combination of literary criticism and moral judgements, he prefaces his *Defence* with an explanation as to why he attempted to "darken" the literary reputation of certain playwrights: "I conceive it very defensible to disarm an adversary, if it may be, and disable him from doing mischief." Following this, 96 of his 139 pages are devoted to a robust and detailed justification of his position in the light of Congreve's *Amendments*. In particular, he spends fourteen pages denying that Congreve's four propositions are "self-evident" or, in Sister Rose Anthony's words, subjecting them "to such rigid scrutiny that they crumble". For example, he seizes upon Congreve's assertion that "the business of comedy is to delight as well as instruct":

> If he means as much, by 'as well', he is mistaken. For delight is but the secondary end of comedy, as I have proved at large.

He is sarcastic about Congreve's claim that a playwright "generally sums up in the concluding lines of the poem [the play's epilogue] the moral of the play":

> 1. This expedient is not always made use of. Examples that lack it are *The Relapse* and *Love in a Nunnery*.
> 2. Sometimes these comprehensive lines do more harm than good: examples of this nature are *The Soldier's Fortune* and *The Old Bachelor*.

3. When the play is lewd, a grave moral amounts to little. The doctor comes too late for the disease, and the antidote is much too weak for the poison.

Almost every one of Congreve's assertions is answered - sometimes with rather more wit than Collier had shown in the *Short View*. One example may suffice. Congreve had boasted of the respectability of his tragedy *The Mourning Bride* by claiming, "If there be immodesty in this tragedy, I must confess myself incapable of ever writing anything with modesty." Collier simply replies: "It may be so."

While Collier admits his error in quoting "wasting" for "wafting", he shows a lawyer's skill in pouncing upon an unguarded remark. Congreve had written of *The Old Bachelor*, "When I wrote it, I had little thought of the stage, but I did it to amuse myself, in a slow recovery from a fit of sickness." If that was an attempt at a light-hearted apologia, it cut no ice with Collier:

What his disease was I am not to enquire; but it must be a very ill one, to be worse than the remedy. The writing of that play is a very dangerous amusement either for sickness or health, or I'm much mistaken.

He then systematically re-evaluates the charges he laid against Congreve: indecent language, "irreligion", abuse of the clergy and the "rewarding" of undeserving characters. For the most part, Collier is more controlled, and therefore more effective, than he was in the *Short View* - although a certain weariness breaks through from time to time:

In earnest, I'm almost tired with answering these things. To strike the air, does but make a man's arm ache.

Refusing to apologise for having "assaulted the town in the seat of their principal . . . pleasure", he again turns to the attack:

I am sorry to hear the encouraging of vice, the liberties of smut, and prophaneness, the exposing of holy things and persons, are such lively satisfactions. The palate must be strangely vitiated to relish such entertainment of this.

He concludes his dissection of Congreve's *Amendments* by pointing out that Congreve had failed to censor two "scandalous" songs from his plays:

This is somewhat unfortunate: one would have thought, if he had neither modesty to make them, nor reason to defend them, he might, at least, have had a little conscience to have given them up.

Collier then turns his attention to Vanbrugh's *Vindication*, reiterating his earlier charges of profaneness, blasphemy, abuse of the clergy and the fact that the undeserving are rewarded, taking Young Fashion in *The Relapse* as a case in point:

> And why so? Has he not provided him a plot, a fortune, and creditable figure? And are not all these signs of good will and inclination? Well, but "his wife is likely to make his heart ache". Indeed so says the Vindicator. But Young Fashion tells another story. He is in no fright about the matter. Upon observing some signs of extravagance in Hoyden, he says to himself . . . "'Tis no matter. She brings an estate will afford me a separate maintenance." This soliloquy . . . teaches the art of marrying the estate without the woman, and makes a noble settlement upon lewdness.

Collier may have proved that vice triumphs in Congreve's plays but, despite this last sally, he was less successful in replying to Vanbrugh. In the main, he falls back on the assumption that evil must not be spoken on the stage, even if it is punished:

> One man injures his neighbour, and another blames him for it. Does this cancel the guilt, and make the fact nothing? One man speaks blasphemy, and another reproves him. Does this justify the boldness, or make the words unspoken?

Collier concludes his *Defence* with responses to just one of the anonymous pamphleteers and to Dennis. That is to say, this November 1698 publication contains no response to several of the anonymous attacks and counter-attacks, nor to any of the September publications. Collier was not responding on the spur of the moment. Others were.

Just three weeks after the appearance of the *Defence*, an anonymous 18-page pamphlet was complaining that "the fruitful Mr Collier, in every page, discovers rancour and a plain desire not to amend but to destroy" and that "Mr Collier has a particular pique against Mr Congreve". On January 1 next, a much longer answer was published. Entitled *The Stage Acquitted*, it was in the form of a dialogue between two fictional characters. Sister Rose Anthony sums up their exchanges:

> For ninety-five pages they ramble on; their arguments are often illogical, their diction is redundant, and their style boring.

She is more scathing of the next contribution to the debate.

Of all the replies evoked by Collier, that of James Drake is the longest and one of the least interesting. It bears the title *The Ancient and Modern*

Stages Surveyed. Or, Mr Collier's View of the Immorality and Prophaneness of the English Stage Set in a True Light. Wherin Some of Mr Collier's Mistakes Are Rectified, and the Comparative Morality of the English Stage is Asserted Upon the Parallel. Although it is superficially anonymous, Collier was later to ascribe it to a Dr James Drake. It is as verbose as its title - 367 pages long - but was later to provoke Collier into a *Second Defence*.

Five more pamphlets and books appeared over the next six months. Then came comparative silence until November 1699 when Dryden commented on the debate in a letter to one Mrs Elizabeth Thomas. This was one of his three responses which we shall consider together later. Meanwhile, in the same month and one year after his first *Defence*, Collier got round to answering Drake (he was presumably busy with his other writing during this period) by publishing his *Second Defence*, or to give it its full title, *A Second Defence of the Short View of the Prophaneness and Immorality of the English Stage, etc., Being a Reply to a Book Entitled "The Ancient and Modern Stages Surveyed, etc."* Collier's work is 142 pages long, and has the date 1700 on its title page but its preface is dated November 26 1699.

Collier is not impressed by Drake:

> His scheme is defective . . . he does not apply his answer to any particulars, nor so much as vindicate one passage accused of indecency and irreligion . . . This author . . . seems to rely more upon stratagem and surprise, than plain force, and open attack. His business is all along to perplex the cause and amuse the reader.

Collier goes on to defend himself with a wealth of quotation from the Early Christian Fathers (Chrysostom, Augustine, etc.) and the classical authors (Tully, Livy, Tacitus, Plutarch and Ovid among others), in the process defending these authors against attacks Drake had made upon them. Sister Rose Anthony summarises the *Second Defence* thus:

> The *Second Defence* shows Collier at boiling point with Drake, caustic in his impatience at the continued resistance of the vindicators of the stage, and tenacious of each and every principle which he had set forth in the *Short View* and in *A Defence of the Short View*.

While the *Second Defence* is very much part of a semi-private war between critics, it does clear up one biographical debating point. Collier did indeed visit the playhouse, for in this *Second Defence* he states, "I must tell him [Drake] I have been there, though not always for diversion."

Early in the following year Daniel Defoe came to the support of Collier, while Colley Cibber, in the Prologue and dedicatory epistle to his comedy *Love Makes a Man*, also referred to the topic. Then Dryden made his two further contributions to the debate, the first being in his Preface to *The Fables*:

> I shall say the less of Mr Collier, because in many things he has taxed me justly; and I have pleaded guilty to all the thoughts and expressions of mine which can be truly argued of obscenity, profaneness, or immorality, and retract them. If he be my enemy, let him triumph; if he by my friend . . . he will be glad of my repentance.

Professor Krutch (among others) has pondered whether Dryden was truly repentant or just conforming to a new ethos in an attempt to regain public favour:

> No one was so fit as he to expose by moderate censure of his time the unfair ferocity of Collier. But perhaps he was too weary to enter into any new controversy. We can never know how sincere was his cry of *mea culpa*, for he died too soon to prove repentance by his works.

But it should be remembered Dryden had written as early as 1685:

> O gracious God! How far have we
> Profaned thy heavenly gift of poesy!
> Made prostitute and profligate the muse,
> Debased to each obscene and impious use,
> Whose harmony was first ordained above
> For tongues of angels and for hymns of love.

In 1699, he had written in similar vein in the letter to Mrs Elizabeth Thomas mentioned above. Mrs Thomas, who apparently had no ambition to be a professional poet, had sent him two of her poems for criticism. In his reply, Dryden offers this warning and apology:

> 'Tis an unprofitable art, to those who profess it; but you, who write only for diversion, may pass your hours with pleasure in it and without prejudice; always avoiding (as I know you will) the licence which Mrs Behn [the playwright Aphra Behn] allowed herself, of writing loosely, and giving, if I may have leave to say so, some scandal to the modesty of her sex. I confess, I am the last man who ought, in justice, to arraign her, who have been myself too much a libertine in most of my poems; which

I should be well contented I had time either to purge, or to see them fairly burned.

However, in the Preface to *The Fables* Dryden also writes (when discussing Chaucer), "A satirical poet is the check of the layman on bad priests." Later, in the same Preface, he turns his attention directly to Collier, pleading guilty but also complaining that Collier has sometimes misinterpreted him and permitting himself to speculate about Collier's motives:

> Yet it were not difficult to prove that in many places he has perverted my meaning by his glosses; and interpreted my words into blasphemy and bawdry of which they were not guilty. Besides that, he is too much given to horse-play in his raillery; and comes to battle like a dictator from the plough. I will not say, 'The zeal of God's house has eaten him up'; but I am sure it has devoured some part of his good manners and civility. It might also be doubted whether it were altogether zeal which prompted him to this rough manner of proceeding; perhaps it became not one of his function [a priest] to rake into the rubbish of ancient and modern plays; a divine might have employed his pains to better purpose than in the nastiness of Plautus and Aristophanes, whose examples, as they excuse not me, so it might be possibly supposed that he read them not without some pleasure.

Dryden repeated this last charge in one of his later poems, *Cymon and Iphigenia*:

> The world will think that we loosely write,
> Tho' now arraigned, he read with some delight;
> Because he seems to chew the cud again,
> When his broad comment makes the text too plain;
> And teaches more in one explaining page,
> Than all the double meanings of the stage.
> What needs he paraphrase on what we mean?
> We were at worst wanton; he's obscene.

Dryden's final comments appear in his Epilogue to *The Pilgrim*. Here he blames not the stage for the immorality of the times but the Court of King Charles:

> Perhaps the parson stretched a point too far,
> When with our theatres he waged a war,
> He tells you, that this very moral age
> Received the first infection from the stage.

> But sure, a banished court, with lewdness fraught,
> The seeds of open vice returning brought.

The infection spread to make cuckolds among the city merchants:

> Thus lodged (as vice by great example thrives)
> It first debauched the daughters and the wives.
> London a fruitful soil, yet never bore
> So plentiful a crop of horns before.

- and only then corrupted the poets and the playwrights:

> The poets, who must live by courts or starve,
> Were proud, so good a government to serve;
> And mixing with buffoons and pimps profane,
> Tainted the stage, for some small snip of gain . . .
> Thus did the thriving malady prevail
> The court its head, the poets but the tail.

If Dryden was not entirely on Collier's side, he nevertheless admitted the validity of some of the latter's accusations.

The other major playwright to engage with Collier was George Farquhar. Born in Londonderry in 1678 and, like Collier, the son of a cleric, he became an actor in Dublin but retired at the age of 20 when he wounded a fellow actor by mistake. He then left Dublin for London - as many another Irish dramatist was to do in later years. He is usually classed as one of the 'Five Great Wits' of the Restoration stage - along with Etherege, Wycherley, Congreve and Vanbrugh. Of his eight plays, the first three were largely unsophisticated and somewhat immoral romps. By 1701, with *Sir Harry Wildair*, he had begun to moralise, either heeding or placating the trend towards "the new morality". *The Twin Rivals* (1702) was a moral melodrama; and by 1707 with his last play *The Beaux's Stratagem*, he was writing in a more sentimental style that pre-echoed the later comedies of the century. Interestingly, the play is set in the provinces - another marked change.

It was in November 1699 that he first made a passing reference to Collier in the epilogue to his play *Love and a Bottle* where he mourns the fact that the stage has lost some of its freedom. Also in 1699, there is a brief allusion to a Collier-type figure in *The Constant Couple*. Towards the end of this play, a city merchant, Alderman Smuggler, confronts his former apprentice Clincher in Newgate Prison. Clincher has turned himself into a beau for which Smuggler berates him:

Smuggler: Ay, sir, and you must break your indentures, and run to the devil in petticoats?

Clincher: Ay, sir, and you must go to the plays, too, sirrah! Lord! Lord what business has a 'prentice at a playhouse, unless it be to hear his master made a cuckold, and his mistress a whore! 'Tis ten to one now, but some malicious poet has my character upon the stage within this month. 'Tis a hard matter now that an honest sober man can't sin in private for this plaguy stage. I gave an honest gentleman five guineas myself towards writing a book against it; and it has done no good, we see.

In 1702, Farquhar gave a fuller, but again indirect, answer to Collier in his *Discourse upon Comedy*. In this he defined comedy as "no more ... than a well-framed tale handsomely told as an agreeable vehicle for counsel or reproof". Reasonable as his argument may have been, it did not answer Collier. Indeed, most of the playwrights' answers were disappointing. As John Loftis has written in *The Revels History of Drama in English*:

Most of the replies elicited by *A Short View*, such as those of Congreve and Vanbrugh, are shrill, petulant and superficial. Tempers were too hot to permit the careful discourse needed to counter such a strong indictment.

And, as we have seen, the mainly anonymous pamphleteers and critics, with the notable exception of Dennis, were less than trenchant. Collier himself was verbose and pompous. He lacked a sense of humour. He was intemperate and prone to sometimes ludicrous exaggeration. So why did the wits of his day fail to defeat his attack?

Three simple truths provide the explanation. First, Collier had a point. As Dryden had admitted, the stage was licentious. It may only have been pandering to the tastes of the Court - but it was "infected". Secondly, and ironically conisdering his own High Church, pro-Stuart, conservative background, Collier had the rising, Protestant middle-class on his side: he happened to articulate the mood of the times. And thirdly, he had defined the parameters of the debate. The playwrights then attempted to answer him in his own style and on his own ground. As Farquhar was later to admit,

The best way of answering Mr Collier was not to have replied at all; for there was so much fire in the book, had not his adversaries thrown in fuel, it would have fed upon itself and so gone out in a blaze.

8

Mr Collier's Dissuasive

On the night of November 26, 1703, a freak tempest ravaged much of northern Europe. It destroyed many buildings, including what had been the Duke's Theatre in Dorset Garden. Back in 1682 the King's and the Duke's companies had amalgamated, the combined company settling in Drury Lane. The Dorset Garden theatre meanwhile had been used increasingly for opera and "spectacular extravagances". On the night of the storm, the production in progress was *Macbeth*. To Collier, it was incontrovertible proof. The theatre was wicked. God was angry:

> Did not nature seem to be in her last agony, and the world ready to expire? And if we go on still in such sins of defiance, may we not be afraid of the punishment of Sodom, and that God should destroy us with fire and brimstone?

That the conjunction of a performance of *Macbeth* "with all its thunder and tempest" - not to mention witchcraft - with a storm might have been coincidence is dismissed by Collier:

> And make us believe the storm was nothing but an eruption of Epicurus's atoms, a spring-tide of matter and motion, and a blind sally of chance? This throwing Providence out of the scheme is an admirable opiate for the conscience!

The fact that the same storm had caused havoc and death all over Europe did not shake Collier's convictions that the London theatres

104

its extensive references to classical authors and over-detailed analysis. Certainly one of the greatest strengths of his *Dissuasive* is its conciseness. In its brief fifteen pages, Collier presents an admirable summary of the arguments he expressed in the *Short View*, though not in the same order.

Just as the *Short View* was in six chapters, the *Dissuasive* contains six main sections. In the first, he condemns the immorality of the stage, again attacking the dramatists for rewarding vice or "representing vice under characters of advantage . . . a finished libertine seldom fails of making his fortune upon the stage". Secondly, Collier attacks "the intolerable profaneness of the stage". He deplores the "making bold with the name of God on the most trivial and scandalous occasions". The dramatists, he maintains, "have blasphemed the attributes of God, ridiculed his providence, and burlesqued the Old and New Testament". Thirdly, he damns the "indecency of the language", "the lusciousness of double entendres" and the absence of "that sobriety of thought proscribed by the Gospels". He discusses the visits of ladies to the theatres, who must either be pleased with the "indecencies of the stage", fail to recognise them as such, or hypocritically deny enjoying the profanity on their frequent and regular visits.

Fourthly, he says, "We must not forget the incorrigibleness of the stage." Laws had been passed, both dramatists and actors prosecuted and the stage was less profane than it once had been, but still Collier discovers licentiousness and profanity. With sudden tolerance, he allows that young people might see one play in their life - under strict supervision. However, he does not maintain it is necessary to visit the playhouse to condemn or criticise it.

Fifthly, he instances civilisations and ecclesiastical authorities which frowned upon the theatre. Sixthly, he summarises his arguments:

> If the stage once gains our fancy, the service of God will grow burdensome and heavy. And when a luscious song becomes relishing, a psalm will be a flat entertainment.

He denies that there can be any point of reconciliation between drama and religion, equating the theatre with the works of darkness. "To frequent the playhouse is plainly inconsistent with the duties and character of a Christian . . . to be present . . . amounts to consent and approbation." Which point leads him to refer to the tempest and the production of *Macbeth*:

Where at the mention of the "chimneys being blown down" the audience were pleased to clap at an unusual length of pleasure and approbation.

Thus Collier concludes his attack and summarises his arguments, convinced of his own position as being one that it is quite impossible to undermine. His *Dissuasive* is nevertheless a key document in the controversy for it gives us an idea of how he himself judged the *Short View* and of what he thought were its key arguments.

This is the text of the pamphlet:

Mr Collier's Private Dissuasive From The Playhouse:
in a Letter to a Person of Quality,
Occasioned by the Late Calamity of the Tempest

Sir,

I remember the last time I waited on you, you expressed a very Christian concern at the disorders of the playhouse; you lamented its having so much the ascendant of the town, and countenance of figure and fortune. You seemed to presage that these nurseries of licence and atheism would, if unrestrained, prove fatal to the nation, make us ripe for destruction, and pull down some terrible vengeance upon our heads. Being thus uneasy in your prospect, and particularly solicitous for the conduct of your family and relations, you were pleased to desire me to draw up something by way of preservative, in as narrow a compass as possible. For, as you observe, in cases of conscience and morality, some people are so frightfully nice and impatient, that you must either cure them extempore, or not at all. The bill must be short, and the medicine quickly swallowed, or else they'll rather die, than come under the doctor.

Sir, waving other reasons of regard for you, your request proceeds from so commendable a motive, that upon this single score I think myself obliged to endeavour your satisfaction.

And here give me leave to suggest to you that, having already in the *View of the Stage* spoken pretty largely to this point, it will be impossible for me to pursue the design without falling upon some of the thoughts of that performance: and since the argument is thus forestalled, your candour (I question not) will make a proportionable allowance.

To begin: the bad complexion, and danger of this diversion, may be set forth,

First, from their representing vice under characters of advantage. Dissolution of manners is the great favourite of the modern muses: to be thorough paced in that which is ill is the chief recommending quality. A finished libertine seldom fails of making his fortune upon the stage. Thus qualified, there is great care taken to furnish him with breeding and address. He is presently put into a post of honour, and an equipage of sense; and if he does the worst, he is pretty sure of speaking the best things - I mean the most lively and entertaining. And all, to hold forth this profitable instruction (for so they must be interpreted) that lewdness and irreligion are the true test of quality, and education. If a man will be just to the interest of reputation, he must throw off the restraints of virtue, set up for a sceptic, and launch boldly into a course of vice. For if he will be brow-beaten by the other world, and over-awed by the whimsies of conscience, this is the way to pass for a clown, to taint his blood, and almost make him disclaimed at the Herald's office! And that this wholesome doctrine may be the better received, the poets have taken care to raise their ban and arrerère-ban [proclamation] upon all that's sacred and solemn, and to persecute virtue under every appearance. And when they make bold with a character of religion, they never fail of showing it clumsy and ridiculous. Such a person must be an original in untowardness, the jest of the company and put into all the disguises of folly and contempt. And when religion is thus bantered, and virtue dressed up in antic, when lewdness appears in circumstances of credit, and makes such a shining figure; when rewards and punishments are under so just a distribution, the government of the stage must needs be surprisingly regular, and improve the audience to admiration!

Secondly, another reason for the *Dissuasive* is the intolerable profaneness of the stage. And here not to mention their swearing in all the excesses of distraction, and making bold with the name of God on the most trivial and scandalous occasions: this, though horrible enough, is the least part of the charge. Their courage on this head is of an amazing size. They are heroes beyond anything upon record, and in a manner perfectly new in their defiance. They have attempted, as it were, to scale the sky, and attack the seat of omnipotence. They have blasphemed the attributes of God, ridiculed his providence, and burlesqued the Old and New Testament. These infernal sallies put me in mind of a late instance of resolution in one of their fraternity; I mean the man that acted *Jephthah's Rash Vow, or the Virgin Sacrifice in Smithfield*. The subject of

the farce is taken out of the book of Judges; and to piece up the entertainment, and it may be to make the history ridiculous, there are several
buffooning characters tagged to the end of it. Now can there be a more
irreligious insolence than to mix the most solemn, and the most ridiculous things together; to prostitute the inspired writings in places of
infamy, and to furnish out a droll from the sacred history? I hope it will
be the last time the Bible will be shown for a sight at Bartholomew Fair.

I am unwilling to say any more upon this matter. To suppose the outrage of such a practice stands in need of satire and aggravation is a
reflection upon the common sense of a nation, and looks as if we were
blasted in our understandings.

Thirdly, the next thing I shall remark is the indecency of their language:
and here the English poets and players are still like themselves. They
strain to a singularity of coarseness: the modern theatres of Europe are
mere vestals to them. They outdo the liberties of Greece and Rome,
the ages of ignorance, and the precedents of heathenism. The lusciousness of double entendres, and remote glances won't serve their turn. To
flash a little upon the imagination, and appear in the twilight, is not
mischief enough. No: they love to have their sense clear and determined:
they labour for perspicuity, and shine out in meridian scandal: they make
the description rank, bring the images close, and show the monster in its
full proportions. And by this stench the spirits are insensibly seized,
and the health of the company often suffers. Thus the impressions of
modesty wear off, the affections are debauched and the memory furnished with ammunition to play upon the conscience. And is this
diversion for Christians? Is this suitable to that holiness of doctrine, to that
sobriety of thought prescribed by the Gospel, or to that taste of satisfaction we expect in the other world? Can the ladies be entertained with such
stuff as this? Those that dress their diet, would make us believe their
palates are strangely out of order. To treat the reservedness of their sex,
their birth and their breeding with smut and ribaldry, is, to speak softly,
incomprehensible manners. In short, it will said, and therefore I shall put
the case: either the ladies are pleased with the indecencies of the stage or
they are not. If they are, 'tis a hard imputation on their virtue; it argues
they have strangely forgotten the engagements of baptism, the maxims
of education; and the regards of their character. 'Tis a sign they are
strongly seized by the infection, and that the tokens are almost ready to
break out. If they are not pleased, it will be enquired why they come there.
Why [do] they venture upon a place where they must expect to have their
imagination shocked, their aversion put into a fit, and their blood called

up into their faces? Who would undergo so much fatigue of fancy and mortification? The playhouse is without doubt the wrong place for discipline; and such penance, if often repeated, will never pass for good earnest. Thus the dilemma bears hard towards the ladies; and for my part, I confess, I have not logic enough to disengage them.

Fourthly, we must not forget the incorrigibleness of the stage. This is a further aggravation of their disorder. Their ill plays have been some of them examined, their licentious extravagance marked, and repeated instances produced upon them. In short, the ulcer has been dissected, the criminals dragged out, and the blasphemy exposed. The poets, 'tis true, rallied upon the defeat, and made the most of their matters. But finding the cause too gross and defenceless, and that the force of truth would prevail, they have since laid down and left the field. But this is not all. The players have met with further instruction: the laws have been let loose upon them; they have been disciplined at Westminster Hall. However, all this conviction and discouragement won't do. They are proof against reason and punishment, against fines and arguments, and come over again with their old smut and profaneness. One would think by their desperate pushing, they were resolved to exterminate religion, and subdue the conscience of the kingdom. And I must needs say, their measures are not taken amiss. They have without doubt pitched upon the most likely expedient to make vice absolute, and atheism universal.

And as if the old batteries were too weak, they have strengthened the attack and levied recruits of music and dancing beyond sea. There was great occasion, no question, to draw down more forces upon flesh and blood and to spring a new mine to help storm the senses, and blow up the passions of combustion! And when people are thus thrown off their guard and disarmed of their discretion, the playhouse is admirably furnished with provision to seize the advantage, and improve the opportunity. For what is it but the common receptacle of vice, and the rendezvous of rakes and strumpets? I don't mean all the company are such. But this I may say, that scarce any quarter is so plentifully stocked. Now who would trust his health in a place of mortality, or go to the pest-house for recreation?

What then, must we never see a play? And where's the harm in it if we don't? Can't we take an ill thing upon report, without the curiosity of experience? Is it not better to stand off from unnecessary danger, than to press upon a formidable enemy and run the hazard of defeat? However, if young people are so uneasy at such a restraint, if they will needs venture, let them fortify themselves at home, and take the guard of religion along with them. Let them go, as they do, to see an outlandish monster, once in their life time. Let the play be prescribed them by persons of conduct and sobriety. In a word, let the snake be frozen, and the poison as much diluted as 'tis possible.

And after all, I don't pretend to give a licence for seeing the playhouse, though under the cautions above mentioned: but if people will rush forward, and stand the event, I only desire to direct the motion and suggest the safest way.

Fifthly, the playhouse has been looked on as a public nuisance, censured and discountenanced by church and state, and that in times both ancient and modern.

To give some instances in the state.

The republic of Rome, before Julius Caesar stopped the building of a theatre, being fully convinced that this diversion would bring in foreign vice, that the old Roman virtue would be lost, and the spirits of the people emasculated. This wise nation made the function of players scandalous, seized their freedoms and threw them out of privilege and reputation.

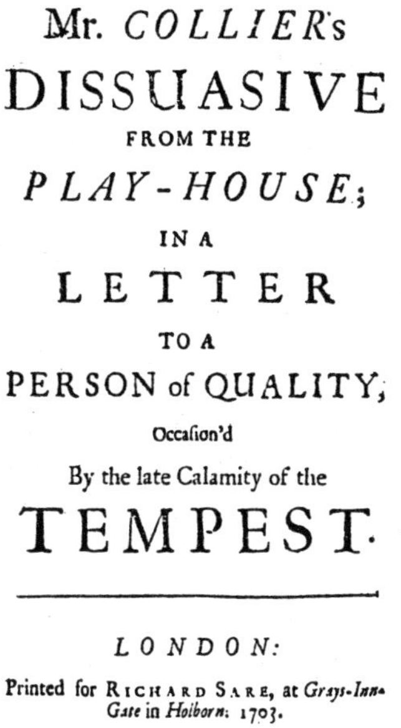

Mr. *COLLIER's*

DISSUASIVE

FROM THE

PLAY-HOUSE;

IN A

LETTER

TO A

PERSON of QUALITY,

Occasion'd

By the late Calamity of the

TEMPEST.

LONDON:

Printed for RICHARD SARE, at *Grays-Inn-Gate* in *Holborn*: 1703.

Figure 5: Mr Collier's *Dissuasive*

To come down to our own constitution: the players are forbidden to act, and scatter their infection through the kingdom, under very severe and infamous penalties. And in the reign of the famous Queen Elizabeth, there was an order of Queen and Council to drive the players out of the city and liberties of London, and to pull down the theatres, which was executed accordingly. In France some few year since, the Italian players were expelled the kingdom, and now the French stage lies under excommunication. The theatres have been lately shut up in Italy by the Pope, and in the territories of Brandenburg by the King of Prussia. And several European countries would never endure them in any form, or under any regulation.

As to the church, the players stand condemned by several councils of great antiquity and credit. And the most celebrated and primitive fathers have declaimed loudly against the stage, with all the zeal, force, and rhetoric imaginable. So that if the strongest precedents, either in church or state, will make any impression upon us; if we have any regard for the wisdom and piety of the best and most considerable part of mankind; if authority will move us; if reason will convince us; if experience will teach us, we have the strongest motives imaginable to stand off from such dangerous ground.

To this I may observe in the sixth place, that such scandalous diversion must of necessity untune our minds, and dispirit our devotion. If the stage once gains our fancy, the service of God will grow burdensome and heavy. And when a luscious song becomes relishing, a psalm will be a flat entertainment. Is it possible for esteem and contempt to stand together, and can we reverence that which has been our sport to see despised? To spend the week at the playhouse, and come to church on the Sunday, looks little better than fashion and grimace. These two places are strangely hostile and counter qualifying: for what communion has light with darkness, and what concord has Christ with Belial? If we sit thus in the seat of the scornful, 'tis in vain to approach his presence and to tread his courts.

And therefore in the last place I shall add, that to frequent the playhouse is plainly inconsistent with the duties and character of a Christian. For, not to repeat what has been said, the guilt of the place must in a great measure fall upon the audience. To be present, after warning, at the abuse of religion, amounts to consent and approbation. To delight in ill company is to become part of it, and all people are principals in profaneness, as well as in murder. Everyone know 'tis the company that supports the playhouse. Without a numerous audience they would be forced to disband, to surrender their business, and, it may be, be discouraged into reformation. What then? Are we to assist such places of liberty and profaneness with our purse and person? Must we keep up the credit of debauchery? Must we make a contribution for blasphemy, and raise a tax for the Government Below? To countenance such practices must inevitably communicate the guilt and heighten the provocation. And when wickedness is thus flaming and outrageous, we cannot expect but that vengeance will quickly follow.

We have lately felt a sad instance of God's judgements in the terrible tempest: Terrible beyond anything in that kind in memory, or record. For not to enlarge on the lamentable wrecks and ruins, were we not almost swept into a chaos? Did not nature seem to be in her last agony, and the world ready to expire? And if we go on still in such sins of defiance, may we not be afraid of the punishment of Sodom, and that God should destroy us with fire and brimstone?

What impression this late calamity has made upon the playhouse, we may guess by their acting *Macbeth* with all its thunder and tempest, the same day: where at the mention of the 'chimneys being blown down', the audience were pleased to clap, at an unusual length of pleasure and approbation. And is not the meaning of all this too intelligible? Does it not look as if they had a mind to out-brave the judgement? And make us believe the storm was nothing but an eruption of Epicurus's atoms, a spring-tide of matter and motion, and a blind sally of chance? This throwing providence out of the scheme, is an admirable opiate for the conscience! And when recollection is laid asleep, the stage will recover of course, and go on with their business effectually.

Thus, Sir, I have laid before you what I have to offer upon this occasion, and am,

Your most humble servant, J. C.　　　　December 10, 1703

Perhaps it had been necessary for Collier to write something as substantial as the *Short View* in order to initiate the debate. The comparatively slender *Dissuasive* might not have attracted the same attention. But it is only because it lacks the unnecessary wealth of illustration present in the *Short View* that it seems lightweight. And since it followed the *Short View*, it was considered by many to be only a reiteration of his earlier arguments. In reality, it is considerably more cogent.

It certainly succeeded in re-opening the debate. Eight further contributions appeared in 1704, as well as the reprint of the *Dissuasive*, seven of them appearing before Easter and five of them instancing the storm as a reason to control or close the theatres. Typical of them is *Some Thoughts Concerning the Stage in a Letter to a Lady*. Published on 19 January 1704, it is ostensibly anonymous but has been credited to one Josiah Woodward who published several works on "the reform of manners". He obviously approves of Collier's writings but also quotes another cleric:

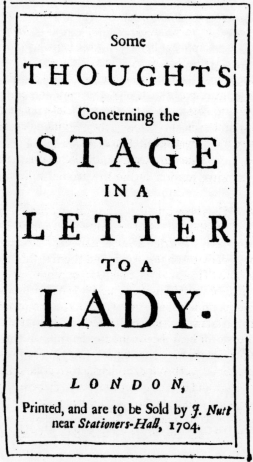

Figure 6: *Some Thoughts Concerning the Stage in a Letter to a Lady*

They [theatre-goers] have so long habituated themselves to the play-houses, that they begin to think a place there to be part of their birthright: but I desire such would be persuaded to hear what the late A B Tillotson thought of these matters, (and I hope some deference is due to his judgement). If they look into the eleventh volume of his sermons, they will find that in his discourse against the evil of corrupt communication, he tells them, 'That plays, as the stage now is, are intolerable, and not fit to be permitted in a civilised, much less in a Christian nation. They do most notoriously minister,' says he, 'both to infidelity and vice. By the profaneness of them they are apt to instil bad principles into the minds of men, and to lessen that awe and reverence which all men ought to have for God and religion: and by their lewdness they teach vice, and are apt to infect the minds of men, and dispose them to lewd and dissolute practices. And therefore,' says he, 'I do not see how any person pretending to sobriety and virtue, and especially to the pure and holy religion of our blessed saviour can, without great guilt and open contradiction to his holy profession, be present at such lewd and immodest plays - much less frequent them, as too many do, who would yet take it very ill to be shut out of the communion of Christians, as they would most certainly have been in the first and purest ages of Christianity.'

Like Collier, he blames the theatre for the storm. Like Collier, he calls for the total suppression of the theatre or, failing that, its strict regulation:

The hand of God has been lifted up against us, we have seen the terrors of the Lord, and felt the arrows of the Almighty; and what can all this mean, but to awaken us to a due sense of danger? And, 'tis to be hoped, the nation has already taken the alarm, and begin to think how to avert God's displeasure. The stage is called in question, and papers are dispersed to warn us of its mischiefs; and it is not improbable that the licentious and unbounded liberty the players have taken of late years, and particularly in their daring to act *The Tempest* within a very few days after the late dreadful storm, has raised in the minds of men such an abhorrence and indignation, that we may possibly be so happy as to see the stage (if not totally suppressed) yet brought under such a regulation, both as to the plays that are acted, and the company that resort to them, that foreigners may no longer stand amazed when brought into our theatres, nor good men tremble at the continuance of them: but that virtue may appear there with all its charms, and vice be exposed to the utmost contempt.

There were those who articulated the opposing view and 1704 saw the publication of two of the most vitriolic and satirical attacks on Collier. One was Tom Brown's play *The Stage Beaux Toss'd in a Blanket* which is the subject of the next chapter; the other was a pamphlet by the critic John Dennis, author of *The Usefulness of the Stage*.

Entitled *The Person of Quality's Answer to Mr Collier's Letter*, it is dated 27 January 1704 and is the most telling response to the *Dissuasive*. Its tone throughout is savagely ironic. Dennis addresses his *Answer* directly to Doctor Collier, claiming to have been so impressed by "your short but divine *Dissuasive*" that he has read it aloud to his family. He first makes the point already quoted that, if Collier is right, "the poor inhabitants of Cologne ... the very Hamburgers and Dantzichers, and all the people of the Baltic, have suffered for the enormities of our English theatres". He continues in sarcastic vein:

The second observation that I made was this, that we have reason to be thankful to heaven, for forbearing us so long. For if the late dreadful judgement had happened in the reign of King Charles II, when the play-houses were licentious in all their impunity, when reformation was so far from being thought of, that the very name was despised and laughed at, what must the dismal consequence not have been? Then we should certainly have been swallowed up; since the judgement was so terrible even the other day, after a five years reformation?

What reason have we to be thankful that we live in an age in which light is come into the world? For in what Egyptian darkness have we lived hitherto! And what a poor reformation was that which was carried on in Queen Elizabeth's time, in comparison of that which you are gloriously projecting? For with that former reformation the playhouse began; grew up and spread and flourished. What a shadow of a reformation was that? 'Tis true popery was driven out, and wholesome laws were enacted to secure the rights of the people. But what signified all that when the playhouse was encouraged? For though, as you learnedly observe, play-houses, in the reign of that great queen, were not permitted to be erected in the liberties of the city, yet in the suburbs they were not only permitted but encouraged with a vengeance; and by whom encouraged? Why not only by the people, but by the Court, nay, by the Council, yes by those poor deluded wretches, Cecil and Walsingham, who believed it to be the business of forsooth wise statesmen to provide honest and reasonable diversions for the people; and at the same time were so infatuated, so were the cause of God's wrath. The critic John Dennis would later mock the illogicality of this belief:

> The divine vengeance which they [the theatres] brought down upon us has involved the very innocent. Not only the poor inhabitants of Cologne, but the very Hamburgers and Dantzichers, and all the people of the Baltic have suffered for the enormities of our English theatres.

At the time of the storm, the Jeremy Collier Controversy seemed to have burned itself out. Following Collier's *Second Defence* at the end of 1699, Cibber, Defoe, Dryden and Farquhar had made their various contributions to the debate. Otherwise, only one other reference to the issue has been discovered from each of the years 1700 and 1701, with three comparatively minor pamphlets being published in 1702. While Sister Rose Anthony reasonably suggests there may have been more, now lost, publications during this period, the controversy, in print at least, did abate.

But the storm was too much for Collier to ignore. He reacted by writing what may have at first been a private letter, addressed simply to a "person of quality". Subsequently printed on 10 December that year as a public pamphlet, *Mr Collier's Dissuasive from the Playhouse* retained its original form: that of a letter to an individual. That Collier was by now a respected public figure is confirmed by the fact that copies of this pamphlet were given away free at church doors on the following 19 June, which was declared a fast day by the recently enthroned Queen Anne, as a sign of national repentance. On that day, "most bishops and clergy of the City of London did in their sermons preach particularly against the notorious profaneness of the play-houses" - according to a later opponent of the stage, Arthur Bedford. The tract given away that day was probably the later, second edition of Collier's *Dissuasive*, dated that month and including an anonymous *Letter by Another Hand*.

The "person of quality" to whom it was originally addressed had apparently "expressed a very Christian concern at the disorders of the playhouse," and Collier makes use of the opportunity afforded by the destruction of the theatre in Dorset Garden to re-express his opinions of the stage. Indeed, it is almost as if Collier had by now recognised some of the weaknesses of the *Short View* - for example, its verbosity, intoxicated, as to believe the entertainments of the theatre not only to be honest and reasonable, but the only honest and reasonable diversions.

Nay the poor mistaken queen herself, encouraged playhouses to that degree, that she not only commanded Shakespeare to write the comedy of the *Merry Wives*, and to write it in ten days time.

[. . .]

When Queen Elizabeth died King James succeeded her; and among the eminent reformers of his reign there was no talk of [condemning] the stage. Nay, on the contrary, to their shame be it spoken, that king and his court appeared to be infinitely delighted with plays. And in his visits to the two universities, plays were the chief of his entertainment.

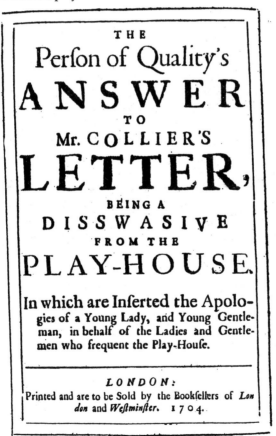

Figure 7: *The Person of Quality's Answer to Mr Collier's Dissuasive*

117

Dennis then turns to the Restoration of 1660:

Well! The King, the bishops and the stage were restored together, and a long time flourished together, without any talk of reforming the playhouses, much less of suppressing them. For the merry ministers of that happy prince laughed at a reformation. And even the former ministers of the church at that time, among whom were certainly some of the greatest men that the Christian world has produced, appeared by no means to be so terribly alarmed at the entertainments of the stage.

His satire is next directed at Collier's refusal to swear the oath of allegiance to the post-Stuart monarchs and his subsequent departure from the official Church of England:

For that you dear doctor, who appear so extremely nice and scrupulous that you dare not so much as take an oath to defend our sovereign lady and us against our mortal enemies; you who are so over cautious that you dare not so much as hold any communion with us; that you should take up this extreme concern for our souls, that you should be so violent for our salvation, is beyond expression wonderful . . . I can never sufficiently admire the excess of your zeal, which is too high and too heavenly to be comprehended by a mortal.

Still in ironic vein, Dennis claims that when a friend attacked Collier, he [Dennis] defended Collier thus:

'Lord sir,' says I, 'you are the most mistaken man in the world. Mr Collier is no such person as you imagine. He is a good natured, sweet tempered man as lives . . . And as for your saying that he has no indulgence for human frailty, why 'tis a sign that you don't know him. 'Tis true, he has taken a fatal aversion to the playhouse; and he will down with it. We have all of us an aversion for something or other. And why should you be so much concerned for that "rendezvous of rakes and strumpets"? But yet Mr Collier has indulgence enough for them too, anywhere but in the playhouse. And where's the mighty hardship then upon them? Are there no places for them to assemble but there? Are there not taverns, brandy shops, coffee houses, chocolate houses, gaming houses for the rakes, and Indian houses [tea shops], music houses, bawdy houses, either for strumpets solitary, or strumpets and rakes in conjunction according as they please? Has Mr Collier writ one word for five years together against any of these places?'

The attack on Collier, now aged 54, becomes personal as the imaginary friend suggests to Dennis what may have prompted the writing of the *Dissuasive*:

'Come, come,' says he, 'I begin to be sensible of the matter. Mr Collier is now declining in years; and the affairs of the world go not according to his wishes. And age and disappointments have soured his blood, and made him loose the relish of sports and gay diversions.'

'Once more,' said I, 'you are the most mistaken man in the world; Mr Collier is far from being a foe to the gayest sports and pastimes; but then he is for having those who frequent them take the consent and approbation of the non-juring clergy along with them, who you know are persons of sobriety and conduct. He'll tell you, that the sports that good Bishop Laud appointed for the Sabbath were not only safe but commendable. That, for example, cricket when it came to be so recommended, immediately became canonical, football orthodox, and jugle-cat, *jure divino* [God's law]. But for the laity to be so impertinent as to choose diversions for themselves; and particularly for the ladies to believe that they have capacities enough to judge between right and wrong, and to distinguish decency from what is not decorum, he takes to be an enormity that is never to be allowed of in any Christian country.

'The playhouse,' said I, 'is one of those which Mr Collier believes to be too luscious a pastime for the laity. To see and to read plays, he thinks is enough, for one of his established virtue. And it must be owned that he has read or seen more than any person in Christendom.'

Dennis next returns to his domestic flight of fancy:

I now come to tell you what has happened upon the receiving your *Dissuasive*; though 'tis scarce three hours since its arrival. Immediately upon the reading it, my eldest son, Jack, told me that he was perfectly satisfied that plays were abominable; and taking his hat, his sword and his cloak, went away for St James's. My eldest daughter, Susan, is gone to take a walk in the Garden, to meditate there in the dark - that she may have the arguments in readiness, by which she says she designs to convert her sister. But my younger son, Charles, made some objections, and so did my daughter, Harriet, which I here send you as well as I can recollect them, because I know, Doctor, that you are able to answer them better than I can.

'Sir,' says Charles, 'I have promised my Lady Freelove today, to wait upon her to the play, and so has my sister Harriet; but for the future I promise you to keep away, and so I dare say will my sister, if you will but answer some objections that we have to make against Mr Collier's discourses.

'I know no reason why Mr Collier should pretend to meddle with our diversions. If he is really offended at plays himself, in the name of God let him keep away. I know nobody who is fond of his company there. But since we don't pretend to oblige him to come, why should he presume to oblige us to keep away?

'If Mr Collier is really offended at playhouses, I would fain know how long he has been so, or what is the reason that he did not write against them when he was young. For the stage was really then more licentious than it is now. Since he forbore writing against them till he was old, we humbly desire that we may not leave them till we are old. And then perhaps we may have some natural or some politic considerations that may oblige us to rail as much as he does.

'How comes this man to take up so much concern for us? Is it Christian charity, and a tender care for our souls? I would fain ask him one question. Is not true religion that which is chiefly necessary for the salvation of souls? If he says it is, why then let me ask him another question. Is the religion which we of the present established Church of England profess the true one, or is it not? If it is, why does not he hold communion with us? If it is not, why does not he set us right? Has he a concern for our souls or not? If he has, why does he not mind the main thing?'

That Collier, while maintaining his moral stance, refused to accept the moral and spiritual authority of the established church, then very much more central to society than it is now, would have struck many of his contemporaries as illogical. Dennis, in the persona of his son Charles, next reiterates a common charge against Collier - and one that has been levelled against many modern moralists and would-be censors:

'But if he is offended at plays, so much as he pretends, why does he see them, why does he read them so much? Why should he be so ridiculously conceited and so spiritually proud, as to think that he can stand under temptations under which we must fall?

'If he has so much aversion for plays as he pretends, if they are so very horrible, why has he read so many? If he really loves them, and they are not so abominable, why has he writ against them?'

'Charles' now acknowledges that the stage has been corrupt but refutes Collier's case that this is a just reason for its abolition, echoing Dennis's earlier defence of pleasure in *The Usefulness of the Stage*:

'Have we spent so much blood and treasure in the defence of our liberties, and shall we suffer an inquisition to be set up for that which is the very life and soul of liberty? And that is harmless pleasure; for 'tis

120

for harmless pleasure we only contend. Let the corruptions of the stage be banished, but let the rest remain.

[. . .]

'Cannot we meet together in a playhouse, where we have no manner of design upon Mr Collier, without alarming him; and raising his passions as he calls it to combustion; when at the same time we have suffered him so long to meet in his separate congregations?'

That is, if members of the Church of England tolerated what by then were seen as the schismatic non-juring congregations, why should not they in turn tolerate those who wish to exercise their freedom to attend theatres?

'It must be acknowledged there are corruptions which are crept into our theatres, for into what human inventions will not corruptions creep, since it is plain that they insensibly creep into religion which is of divine establishment. But it would be a monstrous conclusion that, because of the corruptions of the Church of Rome, revealed religion ought to be suppressed, and men to turn deists or atheists.

''Tis true, there are passages in several of our plays, which I could heartily wish were out. But neither do I see a quarter so many as Mr Collier does, nor do I look upon those which I do see, through his magnifying optics.

[. . .]

''Tis very true sir, as I observed before, that there are several things in our comedies, which I could wish had been left out; and there are particularly some bawdy passages in them, which I wish the authors had had more respect for the audience in general, and for the fair sex in particular, than to have inserted in them. But does he think our virtue so very weak, either the ladies' or the gentlemen's, that we cannot give them a transitory hearing without being debauched by them, while his (it seems) is so very strong that he can dwell for months upon them and make a full collection of them, a collection which has taught several of our ladies more bawdy in two hours, than they would have learned in so many years at the playhouse? Does he believe that nobody ought to entertain them obscenely but himself?'

'Charles' repeats his father's puzzlement that, as a moralist, Collier has confined himself to attacks upon the theatre:

'Does Mr Collier really believe that there is no swearing in gaming houses? No intrigues at India or chocolate houses? No lying, and no [card] sharping in coffee houses, no beastly lewdness at music houses, and bawdy houses? If he believes that these places are guilty of the crimes imputed to them, why does he not preach to them, which have a great deal more occasion for reformation than the playhouse?'

He answers his own question with the accusation that Collier's attack is self-serving:

'What is the reason then that Mr Collier, neglecting the vices of the town, keeps such a bustle at those of the stage? Why, because it is not his design or business to correct or reform anything! His only business is to set up himself: to erect an obscure schismatical parson into a saint of the first magnitude; to pass for a man of more sanctity than all the bishops, and of more discernment than all the ministers of state. His business is not to correct and reform but to amuse, to puzzle, to make a noise and a party.'

He lights upon the inconsistency in the *Short View*: that Collier began by preaching reform and concluded by calling for the abolition of the stage:

'In the beginning of that book, his intent is plainly only to reform the stage. But then afterwards he wisely considered that the obliging the virtuous would not do his business. They are not enough to cry up their champion, and bring him into reputation. But if he appeared an enemy to the stage itself, and attempted to destroy it instead of reforming it, why then he would oblige all the doubty Hectors in virtue, a numerous multitude of false brains who would infallibly stand buff [bear the brunt] for him and be his bully backs [a brothel's bouncer or doorman] on occasion.'

Towards the end of his speech, 'Charles' moves from questioning Collier's motives to questioning his methods:

'If Mr Collier is moved by charity to exclaim thus loudly against the stage, let me ask him one question. Who are the persons whom he designs to reform? They who never come to a playhouse, methinks, should have no occasion for his corrections. If his design is on those who come thither, why does he not insinuate himself into their affections by the meekness and humility of his expressions and the attractive language of charity? Why has he recourse to such presumptuous arrogance, as justly renders him the aversion of some, and the scorn of others?

[. . .]

'But Mr Collier's is the most affected, most foppish style that ever I met with in ancient or modern authors; of which I will undertake to convince any impartial man, if he is but a tolerable judge of writing.'

Then comes a charge, frequently laid against moralists, of hypocrisy - together with what may be, if it is taken at face value, a rare description of Collier:

'I think sir, I have made it plainly appear, that Mr Collier is one who has reason to be afraid of theatres, and therefore to hate them. For he is one of those with a vengeance who endeavour to appear what they are not. And though nowadays a priest is not suffered to be brought upon the stage, yet I question whether he is to be regarded as a priest, who wears a sword of five foot long, and a perruke [wig] of three, and goes about reforming in the same habit, in which the French dragoons are at this very juncture piously "reforming" the Cévennois [in south-east France].'

Once 'Charles' has finished his attack on Collier, Dennis ascribes a further argument to his sixteen-year-old daughter Harriet - thus allowing himself to present a woman's view of the theatre. Dennis tells us, presumably in a deliberately provocative way, that, on hearing the *Dissuasive* read aloud, she became agitated, "the blood began to spring up into her face, her little breasts began to heave and she darted a frown that made her awful even to me, her father".

'He wants logic,' she said. 'Why then, he shall find I have more than he has [. . .]

'The diversions that the town affords, are chiefly reduced to four. 1. Gaming. 2. Music meetings. 3. Balls and meetings for dancing. 4. Going to plays. Now of all these, I am apt to believe that plays are the most innocent for the following reasons. They raise the passions only to correct them, whereas the others raise them merely for the sake of inflaming them. The plays, and more especially tragedies instruct us in virtue, which the other diversions do not. They improve us in lawful innocent knowledge, which in some measure supplies the want of education in our sex. They form our language and polish our minds and so capacitate us, when we come to marry to engage and endear our husbands to us ... Sir, in short the case is thus. Diversions the ladies of a great metropolis must have. I have particularised the several diversions which this town affords. All the danger, and all the temptation which this judicious person supposes to be at the playhouse, are really in all the other diversions which have none of the advantages that may be reaped from tragedies, for the improvement either of our virtue or knowledge. Why then would this mighty reformer have us leave plays for them?

[. . .]

'True sir, there are passages in some of our plays which I could heartily wish were out. But does he think the virtue of the ladies who frequent playhouses is so very weak, as to be overthrown by the lusciousness, as he calls it, of a scribbler's double entendres?'

Having allowed his daughter to complete his case, Dennis flamboyantly concludes his *Letter* or pamphlet with news of his more "moral" children - Jack and Susan, who had, as he told us earlier, rejected the stage in favour of entertainments Collier had not damned:

News is brought me from Piccadilly that Jack has lost a thousand pound at picket [a card game], and Susan who went into the Garden forsooth to meditate, though she went out as black as a raven, being in mourning for her great aunt yet, as I hope for mercy, the jade [hussy] is returned as white and as powdered [like a prostitute] as if she had been hard at work in a bolting-house [where flour is sifted]. So that I could wish that for this one night they had both been with Harriet and with Charles at the 'Tabernacle of the Wicked'.

Despite such defences and the satire of Thomas Brown (see Chapter Nine), the reformation of the stage had begun (see Chapter Ten).

9

The Stage Beaux Toss'd in a Blanket

The lines for which the author of this play, Thomas Brown (1663–1704), is chiefly remembered were written while he was a student at Christ Church, Oxford. His subject was the college dean, who was also Bishop of Oxford, Dr Fell:

> I do not love you, Doctor Fell;
> But why, I cannot tell;
> But this I know full well,
> I do not love you, Doctor Fell.

In fact, Dr Fell deserves to be remembered for his work in promoting and developing the Oxford University Press. Thanks to Brown, he has simply given his name to any "vaguely unamiable" person.

On leaving Oxford, Brown settled in London and earned a living as a hack writer, satirist and translator, his languages being Latin, French, Italian, Spanish and Greek. Brown's *Amusements Serious and Comical* (1700) are a series of entertaining sketches of London life. His *Collected Works* were published posthumously in two volumes in 1707, with a third volume added in 1708.

It was in the year of his death that he published his venomous satire on Collier. Its full title is *The Stage Beaux Toss'd in a Blanket; or*

Hypocrisie . . . à la mode. The title page added the following: *"Exposed in a True Picture of Jerry ------- A Pretending Scourge to the English Stage."* Printed with the text of the play was an epistle dedicatory to one Christopher Rich, Esq. - described as a patentee (licensee) of the Theatre Royal. Also included were a prologue to the play - "being a full explanation of the . . . doctor's book" - and an epilogue "on the reformers", both having been spoken at the Theatre Royal.

So far as is known, the play itself was not acted at the time of publication and has never since been performed. One bibliography describes it as "unacted and not intended for performance". Others might say it is unactable. Certainly it is remarkably static, the second act being simply a debate on stage reform in which the various arguments are rehearsed. The play, running to some sixty pages, consists of three acts in all, the third revealing Jerry as a fornicating hypocrite.

It would of course have been libellous had Jerry been more overtly described as the Reverend Jeremy Collier. Instead, the Collier figure is described as Sir Jerry Witwoud - though many of this character's speeches are quoted directly from the *Short View* and from Collier's *Defence of the Short View*. Several of the other characters' arguments echo other contributions to the debate, for example, Dennis's *Usefulness of the Stage* and Vanbrugh's *Short Vindication*. Despite Sir Jerry obviously representing the author of the *Short View*, Collier himself is mentioned unflatteringly in the course of the play.

Brown describes his play's characters thus:

Urania - A lady of quality and good sense, gay in her humour, a lover of company, and free in her conversation, of true honour and virtue, a friend of the stage.

Eliza - Her friend and cousin, something more reserved and who, though she loves company, is more nice in the choice of it; a lady of honour, sense, and religion, a friend to the stage.

Dorimant - A man of sense and sound judgement, virtue and honour, of true morals and religion, a friend to the stage because it promotes virtue by exposing fools, fops and knaves.

Hotspur - An earnest foe to hypocrisy and coxcombs; a man of virtue, honour, religion and good sense; and a zealous friend to the stage, because it promotes virtue by exposing fops and knaves &c.

Clemene - An affected hypocrite, coquette and jilt, and one whose reputation has not been without notorious blemishes in the very eye of the world, and yet continues no enemy to the cause of her lost reputation, by hoping now to secure herself under a noisy railing at vice, pretends to be a professed enemy to the stage since the publishing [of] Mr Collier's book; an admirer of Sir Jerry Witwoud.

Lord Vaunt-Title - Vain of his quality, a smatterer in poetry, who having his plays refused, turns enemy to the stage, and condemns the poets for bringing in Lords sometimes as fools.

Sir Jerry Witwoud - A pert, talkative, half-witted coxcomb, vain of a very little learning, always swims with the stream of popular opinion, a great censurer of men and books, always positive, seldom or never in the right, a noisy pretender to virtue, and an impudent pretender to modesty, a hypocrite, and false zealot for religion, and sets up for a reformer of the stage, of a sagacious nose in finding out smut or obscenity; a wonderful artist at extracting profaneness out of all things that fall into his hands; a professed enemy of the stage, though a frequenter of it; once thought a divine, but for reasons best known to himself he has cast his gown for the vanities of a beau wig and sword; vain, proud, ill-natured, and incapable of conversation.

The first act of the play is reproduced here to convey its nature and style. Some short cuts have been made and are indicated by [...]. As elsewhere in the quotations reproduced in this book, the punctuation has been modernised to facilitate the reading of the text.

Act I Scene One

*Scene: a room. Enter **Urania** and **Eliza**.*

Urania: No visitants yet, cousin? This is very strange.

Eliza: That neither of us have had so much as one all this while, I confess is something uncommon, when your house is the constant rendezvous of all the young and gay of the town.

Urania: I own I have thought the time since dinner tedious enough in all conscience.

Eliza: To me, on the contrary, it has seemed extremely short.

Urania: Oh, cousin! Good wits love to be alone.

Eliza: Ah, madam! I'm the wit's very humble servant, but you know my pretences to wit are but very slender.

Urania: The less you pretend, the more is your right, cousin. But, for my part, I avow my love of conversation and society! Solitude is a kind of effect of self-love, and may be excusable, where there are beauties to feed the vanity; but I find so little in myself to please myself, that I'm forced to call in the auxiliaries of good company to drive away so unpleasing an invader.

Eliza: Nay, my good cousin, I am not so smitten with myself neither, as to be an enemy of conversation. Nature has made us for society, and there's no living without it. And as she has made it necessary, so am I far from thinking it disagreeable. But then I'm for a chosen company, that which is select and picked, not promiscuous. I hate the impertinent visits of fools and fops, of the crafty, close and designing - of both sexes, that put us on a painful guard, and pervert the pleasure into a business. 'Tis that medley of company which you receive, that makes it so pleasing to me to be sometimes alone.

Urania: Your delicacy is too refined and your palate too nice, if you can relish the conversation of none but people of sense.

Eliza: And your complaisance too general, that can admit indifferently of all sorts!

Urania: The reasonable gratify my understanding, the fantastic my mirth. I relish the witty, and laugh at the fools.

Eliza: A fool diverts but once, the second visit must be nauseous. Who more than once would hear my Lord Vaunt-Title's ridiculous harangues on quality? Or Sir Jerry Witwoud's awkward love or scandal? His lordship's heavy poetry? Or the knight's heavier criticisms?

Urania: On women, dress, and plays?

Eliza: On the first he's more severe than an old maid of sixty who owes her celibacy to her lost reputation; nicer on the second than a solemn cox-comb just arrived from France; on the last more ill-natured than an exploded poetaster.

Urania: Nay, my lord and he are enemies to women, good dress, and plays with good reason, being laughed at by the ladies, shunned and pointed at by the men, and exposed by the stage.

Eliza: Nay, the playhouse, I confess, they ought to abhor, since they so often see their own ugly faces there.

Urania: The stage-glass is not made to flatter fools and knaves [. . .]

Eliza: Lord! Can't they forbear looking in it, if they are frightened at their own faces?

Urania: Or can't they correct their follies if they find them so disagreeable?

Eliza: Oh! Never cousin, never. A fool is always too fond of his own judgement to own his error by quitting his folly, and the knave finds too much the sweet of his roguery to discard it at the expense of his interest; and their

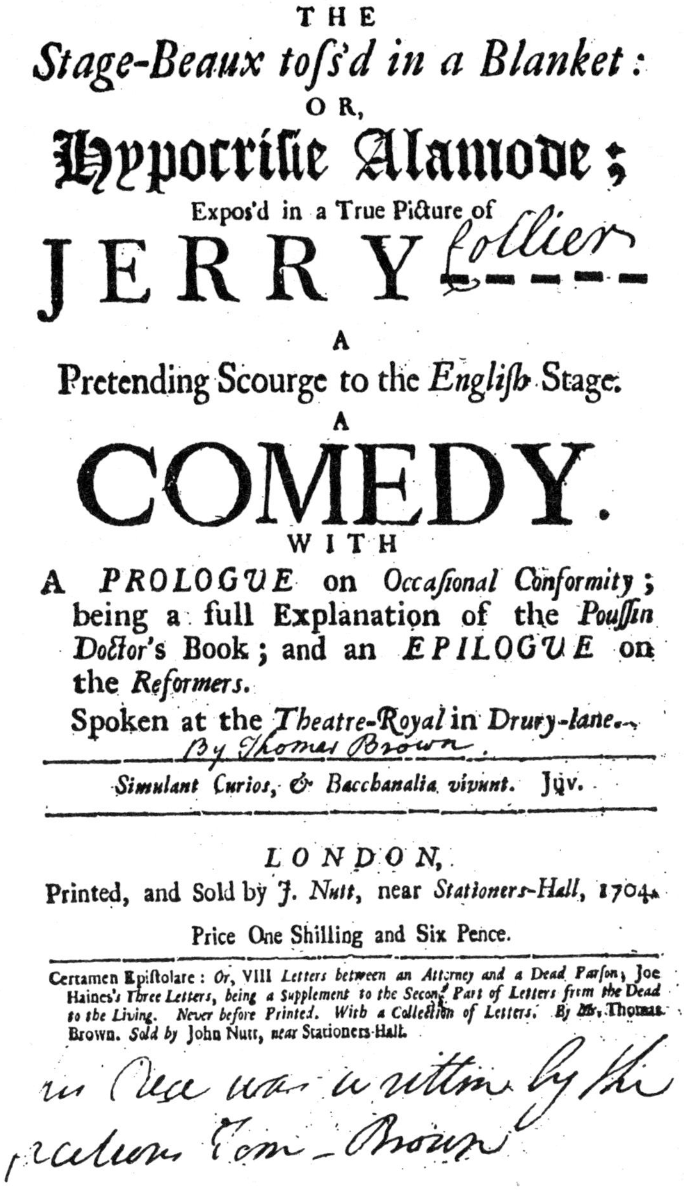

THE

Stage-Beaux tofs'd in a Blanket :
OR,

Hypocrifie Alamode;

Expos'd in a True Picture of

JERRY *Collier*

A

Pretending Scourge to the *English* Stage.

A

COMEDY.

WITH

A *PROLOGUE* on *Occafional Conformity* ;
being a full Explanation of the *Pouffin*
Doctor's Book ; and an *EPILOGUE* on
the *Reformers.*
Spoken at the *Theatre-Royal* in *Drury-lane.*
By Thomas Brown.

Simulant Curios, & Bacchanalia vivunt. Juv.

LONDON,
Printed, and Sold by *J. Nutt,* near *Stationers-Hall,* 1704.

Price One Shilling and Six Pence.

Certamen Epiftolare : Or, VIII *Letters between an Attorney and a Dead Parfon,* Joe
Haines's *Three Letters, being a Supplement to the Second Part of Letters from the Dead
to the Living. Never before Printed. With a Collection of Letters. By Mr. Thomas*
Brown. Sold by John Nutt, *near* Stationers-Hall.

Figure 8: The Stage Beaux Toss'd in a Blanket

129

real quarrel to the stage is not that it shows their pictures deformed to themselves, but to everybody else.

Urania: I dare say this is the greatest pique his Lordship, the knight and some others have to it. Their follies and vices are too conspicuous, and too well beloved, not to engage them in the squabble.

Eliza: How can you then admit of their visits?

Urania: Because everybody else does, and I hate to be singular. 'Tis always the effect of pride, ill-nature, or hypocrisy. Equipage and title takes away all blemishes, for 'tis only the poverty of the fool, or sinner, not the folly or the guilt, that makes a fop, or debauchee, scandalous, or to be shunned. Besides, I have ordered myself to be denied, but the familiar things will take no denial. I know no way but making my footmen turn 'em out of doors, and that's a remedy worse than the disease. But why do we preposterously trouble ourselves with their impertinence, when we have the good fortune to be free from their visits? I wonder Dorimant is not come yet, when he promised to be here betimes, to give us a character of the last new play, and sup with us?

Eliza: Ten to one he has forgot it. Men naturally forget an appointment. When virtue is the only prospect of the assignation, the only dish they are invited to.

Urania: Not men of Dorimant's sense and virtue. Eliza, a man of sense knows there is no merit in vice, and whatever folly may betray him to the conversation of the weak and dishonest of our sex, he easily finds that there can be no sure satisfaction in friendship where there is no virtue.

Enter a Page.

Page: Madam, my Lady Clemene is come to wait on your ladyship.

Urania: Heaven forbid! My dear Eliza, who can bear this killing visit?

Eliza: A just judgement on you, cousin, for your complaint of solitude.

Urania: Run, run down immediately, and tell her I'm not at home.

Page: I have told her already that you are, madam.

Urania: You heedless little animal you, what have you done?

Page: Who I, madam?

Urania: I'll have you better taught than to give answers on your own head.

Page: I'll run down and stop her - I'll tell her that your ladyship is not pleased to be at home. *(Going.)*

Urania: Stay, you thoughtless thing, you - you've done mischief enough already.

Page: Why, madam, 'twill time enough, for when I came up she was engaged in a dispute with a lord, whose coach was passing your ladyship's door when her's stopped.

Urania: Go, get you down, and wait on her up - Oh! My Eliza! How shall we support the fatigue of this visit?

Eliza: Nay, I confess the lady is naturally a little fatiguing, and my aversion of all aversions, as Olivia says, and I think her (with respect to her quality, be it spoken) one of the most insipid monsters that ever pretended to arguing.

Urania: Your expressions, my dear, is a little too gross.

Eliza: Not one jot - no, no - 'tis no more than her due. Nay, much less, if I did her justice. Oh! She's the most intolerable of impertinents.

Urania: That she most exclaims at.

Eliza: She may exclaim at the name as much as she pleases, she is most visibly the thing; for in short she is from head to foot the most affected creature alive. She looks as if her whole body were out of joint, her shoulders, hips and head, moving like clockwork on springs. She affects a continual languishment of voice when she speaks, and is perpetually simpering and rolling her eyes, to court the reputation of a little mouth and full eyes.

Urania: Not so loud - should she come up and overhear us . . .

Eliza: Oh, never fear, she comes not yet - her mind's as affected as her body. She struggles hard to a reputation of wit and religion, but her awkwardness betrays her hypocrisy and folly: she supplies the necessities of a bankrupt reputation and a loose life, with the easy composition of noise and nonsense.

Urania: No more - I hear her - I'll receive her at my chamber door.

Eliza: But one word, and I've done - I'd fain have her married to the lord we mentioned just now; there's such a near relation betwixt their understanding their virtue and their folly that the union must needs be extraordinary.

Urania: Hold your tongue! See, she's here. *(Enter Clemene.)* Oh, madam, how long 'tis since . . .

Clemene: Eh! Mee dear excuse me! Let me see if I'm not just dead! Oh, a chair immediately!

Urania: Page, a chair quickly.

Clemene: Eh ged! Eh ged!

Urania: Ah, madam! What's the matter?

Clemene: Eh! I'm quite spent!

Urania: What will you have?

Clemene: Eh! Eh! My heart is beating its last!

Urania: The vapours?

Clemene: No, no . . .

Urania: Will you be unlaced?

Clemene: Eh ged! No - Eh!

Urania: What's your distemper?

Eliza: How long have you been ill?

Clemene: Eh! I have been above these three hours at that filthy place. Eh!

Eliza: What filthy place, madam, could your ladyship go to?

Clemene: I protest I'm ashamed to name it. Eh!

Urania: How, madam!

Clemene: Nay, but my Lord Vaunt-Title and Sir Jerry Witwoud carried me by main force. Let me dee! It was a perfect rape on my understanding.

Eliza: Pray, madam, explain yourself.

Clemene: Eh! That school of debauchery, the playhouse, medem! Let me dee, if I have [ever] been there since the charming Mr Collier's book came out, before. And now for my sins, madam, for my sins, was I buried to that sink of profaneness and smut. But it has given me the palpitation of the heart so violently, that let me dee, I shan't recover it this fortnight.

Eliza: Ah, cousin! The misery of human life! How strangely diseases fall on us which we never dream of!

Clemene: And then - which is the biggest misfortune of all, madam, let me dee, if I did not just at your ladyship's door meet my Lord Truewit's coach [. . .]

Urania: I own, madam, I don't know what sort of strong constitution my cousin and I are made of, for we were there twice this week, and yet came home safe and sound, easy pleased, and gay.

Clemene: Eh! Madam, and are you one of the abandoned? Do you see plays too?

Urania: Yes, and mind 'em too.

Clemene: And do they not put you almost into convulsions?

Urania: I thank my stars I'm not so nice; and for what I can find by plays, they're more likely to cure than make us sick.

Clemene: Eh! Madam! What is it you say? Can any person, that is a person of the least revenue in understanding, advance such an extravagant absurdity? Can a lady [. . .] run so directly on the point and edge of reason, without any apprehension of a wound and is there in reality any person of sense who is so very hungry and greedy after laughter, as to be able to relish the nauseous impertinencies of plays? Eh! For my part, I avow myself insensible of the least grain of wit in any of 'em. They all provoke me in the most furious degree of disgust, and even sickness at everything in them.

Eliza: Ah! With what a charming eloquence my lady speaks! I swear I thought a play a good, innocent, useful, entertainment! But she has so persuasive an art, and gives what she says so agreeable a turn, that we can't resist our inclinations to side with her opinion.

Urania: I'm not so full of complaisance to sacrifice my opinion to another's humour, without conviction: and till I have better reasons than any of the party have yet urged, I shall think well of the stage.

Clemene: Eh! Let me dee, medem! If I have not the least pity for you - take my opinion me dear, and recall the deviations of your judgement, let not the world, the censorious world, know that ever the filthy odious plays could please you.

Eliza: Ah, cousin! How gay and engaging is the very manner and air of my lady's discourse? The very dress ravishes, but the sense transports. How I pity the poor players, who have so powerful an enemy.

Clemene: Eh! The hideous obscenity and ordures of the plays!

Urania: Sure, madam, your ladyship's smell has a peculiar turn that way! For I protest I can discover no such matter!

Clemene: No, no, my dear, you shall never persuade me to that - but you are one of the obstinate ones who though convinced, think it a scandal to own your error - for let me dee, medem, if the filthy poets do not leave the odious things so open and barefaced, that there's not so much as a lawn veil drawn over them to justify the beholders, but the beastly nudities are so very monstrous and visible, that the most prostituted eyes in the universe can't look that way without blushes and confusion [. . .]

Urania: Pray, madam, be particular - point out some of these ordures, as you can 'em.

Clemene: Eh! Madam, is there then a necessity of being particular?

Urania: Yes, where the case is doubtful.

Clemene: Eh!

Urania: Come, pray be particular.

Clemene: Eh! Fie!

Urania: I beg you.

Clemene: Eh! Madam, you call all the blood in my body to my face! I'm in the last confusion, I've not one word to say to you!

Urania: I'm ignorant of the cause, being not able to discover these ordures myself.

Clemene: So much the worse for you.

Urania: So much the better rather in my opinion. I only take things to be what they are offered for, nor give myself the immodest fatigue to rack and torture an expression to confess a guilty sense which the poet neither exposed to my view, or meant.

Clemene: A woman's modesty!

Urania: A woman's modesty lies not in grimaces and affectation of knowing more in those particulars than other people; this affectation is the worst symptom in the world of a sick mind, and there can be no modesty in the world so ridiculous as that which takes everything in the worst sense. It discovers what hypocrisy would conceal, for it must argue a very good acquaintance with the lady to know her in a mask and disguise, and that at first sight.

Clemene: In short, madam, you may say what you please - but all plays are full of insupportable ordures.

Eliza: That's a most charming word, madam, I don't know what it means, yet certainly 'tis the most ravishing word in the world.

Clemene: In fine, madam, you see your own cousin takes my part.

Urania: Ah! Madam, if you dare believe me, you should not build much on that, since she's a dissembler, and won't speak her mind.

Eliza: Oh, fie, cousin - be not so mischievous to bring me into suspicion with my lady! Should she give credit to your calumny, how unfortunate should I be! I hope, madam, I lie under no such injurious thoughts from your ladyship.

Clemene: No, no, me dear, I mind her not, and believe you more sincere.

Eliza: Madam, you're infinitely in the right, and you do me but justice when you believe. I think you one of the most accomplished and engaging persons alive; that I'm entirely vanquished by your reasons, am absolutely of your sentiments, and extravagantly charmed with every expression you utter.

Clemene: [. . .] Madam, I speak without affectation.

Eliza: That's apparent, medem! As that all you say and do is natural and easy, your words, the tone of your voice, your mien, your actions, your address, has I know not what of quality in them, which charms every beholder. I'm studying every motion of your eyes and mouth; and I'm so full of you, medem, that the town in a little time will take me for a very counterfeit of your ladyship.

Clemene: Eh! Medem, you mock me!

Eliza: How can you think me so stupid?

Clemene: Let me dee, medem, I'm but a scurvy model.

Eliza: The best in the world, medem.

Clemene: Eh! You flatter me, me dear!

Eliza: Not in the least, medem!

134

Clemene: Spare my blushes I conjure you, medem.

Eliza: Eh! Medem, I've spared you extremely, for I've not said a quarter of what I think.

Clemene: Eh! Medem! Ged, medem no more. You've put me into a most inexpressible confusion - in short, medem Urania, we are two to one, and obstinacy and opiniatietures, you know, are so unworthy a woman of wit.

*Enter **Lord Vaunt-Title** at the chamber door struggling with the **Page**, who would stop him.*

Page: Pray, sir, go no farther!

Lord Vaunt-Title: Sure you don't know me!

Page: Yes, my lord, I do - but you are not to come in.

Vaunt-Title: What brutal insolence is this?

Page: My lord, don't call your civility in question by forcing into a lady's apartment whether she will or not.

Vaunt-Title: I come to wait on your lady.

Page: But my lady, sir, will not be waited on - I told your lordship that she was not within.

Vaunt-Title: Why, I see her in the room there.

Page: That's true, my lord - but yet I tell you she is not within.

Urania: What's the matter there?

Vaunt-T: Only your ladyship's page is for playing the fool a little, madam.

Page: I told my lord that your ladyship was not at home, and yet he would needs press into the room.

Urania: And why did you tell my lord so?

Page: Because your ladyship was angry last time for letting him know that you were within.

Urania: Was ever such impudence in so young a creature! I hope your lordship has a better opinion of me than to believe what he says; he takes your Lordship for an impertinent dancing-master I cautioned him about.

Vaunt-Title: Oh! Medem, I'm infinitely satisfied of the truth of what you say, and in respect of your ladyship I shall forbear to teach him to distinguish better betwixt a man of quality and a dancing-master.

Eliza: There's an obliging difference, cousin!

Urania: A chair there, impertinent.

Page: There is one madam.

Urania: Reach it my lord.

*The **Page** thrusts it rudely to him.*

Vaunt-Title: Your page, medem, has a strange aversion to my person.

Eliza: He's much in the wrong, my lord.

Vaunt-Title: I fancy my ill mien is not engaging enough with him!*(Laughs.)*
But, pray ladies, what were you upon?

Urania: The playhouse, my lord.

Vaunt-Title: I just came from it.

Eliza: With this lady.

Vaunt-Title: Right, madam, she did me the honour to sacrifice three hours
to the adornment of the boxes, for rat me if there has not been a dearth of
beauty there ever since her ladyship has forsaken the house, except when
your ladyship was there.

Clemene: Well, my lord, your opinion of the playhouse.

Vaunt-Title: Rat me, a most impertinent place.

Clemene: Eh! How I am ravished with your judgement, me lord!

Vaunt-T: Oh! 'Tis the most abominable insipid place, rat me, in the universe! Why, medem, the devil take me if I was not horribly squeezed to
get a place there! I thought I should have been smothered or pressed to
death to get in. See how hideously my clothes and peruque are, and
rumpled; by your favour, lady, I must adjust me. *(Goes to the glass.)*

Eliza: Nay, that indeed ought to cry vengeance on the place, and justifies
your lordship's censure.

Vaunt-Title: And then the vulgar rascals share with quality in the diversion, the very footmen in the upper gallery will judge of the plays as
well and louder than their masters, though indeed the beastly things are
fit for none else to see.

Urania: Why how has the stage offended your lordship?

Vaunt-Title: Rat me, medem, the saucy rogues that tread it would not act
a play I wrote for my diversion, unless I'd secure them they should not
lose by it.

Clemene: That indeed was an insupportable affront.

Vaunt-Title: And then, medem, the parts are so impudent sometimes
to make a lord a fool.

Urania: That's no reflection on the lord that has wit and sense.

Vaunt-Title: Rat me if I would not have them drubbed, but that it would
cost me money.

Enter Sir Jerry Witwoud.

Sir Jerry Witwoud: I beg your pardon, madam, for so late a visit. But since
the play I was hurried away by a couple of poets of quality, to hear two
lampoons, two ditties, and some other madrigals, which I've forgot
already.

Clemene: I warrant they were hideous creatures, Sir Jerry, that you could
not stay no longer with them.

Sir Jerry Witwoud: They were the top of the extraordinary private scribblers, that always communicate their own writings in a third person's name, that they may have the liberty of praising them the more, and indeed deserve the upper end of all the coxcombs in town. Their poetry was like a bitch over-stocked with puppies, the litter of [which] was so large, that they sucked the sense to the skin and bone. I look upon a man capable of but four big misfortunes - ill dress, no money, scribbling without learning, and living without a belly-passion; and of these four which do your ladyship think the three biggest?

Urania: Oh! The three first without dispute, Sir Jerry.

Wit: And of these three were both these sparks most rampantly guilty; they had the cacoethes [incurable itch] of scribbling without learning, dressing without genius, and running in debt without any money to pay; it's empty of wit as a modern comedy, as ill dressed as a temple beaux, and as poor as - as - as a disbanded ensign, or college servitor.

Clemene: But, Sir Jerry, this company's divided about the playhouse, your opinion may decide the dispute.

Witwoud: The very mark of the beast is on it, 'tis scandalously rampant in smut and profaneness.

Clemene: Do you hear that, madam? Sir Jerry is a scholar, and he declares for me.

Urania: Opinion and vogue, madam, has seldom any force on me, if reason be against them. Reason and evidence can never lose their excellence, because a faction run on in a cry, that has been artfully raised by mean designs, only to gratify a private gain by a public injury.

Witwoud: Madam, when I say it, you may satisfy yourself I have reasons enough for my assertion.

Enter Dorimant.

Urania: Oh! Dorimant, you are come to my assistance in a lucky minute, and bring Right, a better advocate than a woman.

Dorimant: Not than such a woman as your ladyship, madam; but I pray ladies and gentlemen keep your places, nor let me interrupt your discourse, for you are on a subject that has long divided the town.

Urania: Here's my lord's a violent enemy of the stage.

Vaunt-Title: True, medem, I am so - for it's contempt of quality. In short, it is a most detestable place; refuse me, detestable to the last degree; more detestable than anything that can be called detestable.

Dorimant: My judgement and reason then are most detestable.

Vaunt-T: Why, rat me, Dorimant, dost thou pretend to defend it?

Dorimant: Yes, my lord, I am that bold man - but pray, my lord, what are the reasons of your indignation?

Vaunt-Title: Reasons why the stage is detestable?

Dorimant: Yes, my lord.

Vaunt-Title: It is detestable because it is detestable.

Dorimant: After this indeed, who would say one word more - the sentence is past, and the pulpit without any more ado condemned.

Vaunt-Title: Sir Jerry here's of my mind.

Dorimant: The authority is admirable, I confess.

Witwoud: And are you a defender of the stage?

Dorimant: Certainly, Sir Jerry.

Vaunt-Title: Demme, I'll take care to inform the poor rogues of their advocate. *(Laughs.)*

Clemene: Eh! Let me say, Mr Dorimant, this is furiously incongruous to your reputation, for Mr Collier has proved the poets a company of strange debauched fellows, who are furiously my aversion.

Dorimant: Mr Collier does by the poets, what he says Aristophanes did by Socrates: he puts them on an odious dress, and then rails at them for their habit. But what say you if I am persuaded to be for the stage, even by your beloved Mr Collier?

Clemene / Vaunt-Title / Witwoud: *(Laughing)* That's pleasant indeed!

Clemene: Eh! Mr Dorimant, you are for paradoxes to shew your wit!

Dorimant: I am for truth, madam - and what I say I give my reason for - he tells us in the very front of his book, that the business of the stage is to recommend virtue, and discountenance vice, to show the uncertainty of human greatness, the sudden turns of fate, and the unhappy conclusions of violence and injustice, to expose the singularities of pride and fancy, to make folly and falsehood contemptible, and to bring everything that is ill under infamy and neglect. After this, who would not be for the stage, that dares pretend to be a lover of either virtue or sense?

Witwoud: But you forget this cloud of authorities against it.

Dorimant: Authorities! Against what, Sir Jerry? Against the most efficacious means the wit of man can invent for the promoting virtue, and discouraging vice? What signifies authorities against reason? But he has omitted some things which our stage does of equal value with what is mentioned - it ridicules hypocrisy and avarice, the first ruining religion, the latter the state; so that the stage is the champion of the Church and State, against the invasions of two of their most formidable enemies; and this is what renders it odious to those who cry out against it. It is not that it is lewd, profane, or immoral, but because it exposes the vices and follies of a too prevailing party, the hypocrites, and misers.

Clemene: Eh! Ged! Mr Dorimant, and don't you think that the stage is guilty of smut, profaneness and blasphemy?

Dorimant: I think some poets have been guilty of some of these faults, but from a particular to a general there is no arguing. And the Goliath adversary of the stage would not allow it in his own case, because there has been profaneness and blasphemy in some particular pulpits, therefore the pulpit is profane and blasphemous. But I should be tedious to say all I could from your chief stage accuser.

Clemene: Eh! Sir, pray go on - say all you have to say, and then have the mortification, let me say, to see that one line of Mr Collier is more prevailing than all your harangues . . .

Dorimant: Ah! Madam - I'm ready to sacrifice my reason to your opinion, and make the stage submit to your resentment without one word more in its defence . . .

Clemene: Eh! Ged! Mr Dorimant, you're too complaisant. No, no, take your own sentiment, I would not owe my victory to my eyes, but my reason.

Eliza: No, no - my lady is more spiritual, Mr Dorimant, you'll find it a hard matter [. . .]

Dorimant: Why, madam, how long have you been of her opinion?

Eliza: My lady here by her admirable reasons and engaging manner has won me to her side since this dispute began, therefore I'll have no private parley with the foe - but since my lord and I have not much to say in the controversy, we have the better opportunity of conversing on a more agreeable subject.

Clemene: Lerd, madam, my lord indeed is a perfect master of the art of love.

Eliza: Your ladyship speaks sensibly of his lordship's perfections - but I assure you, medem, his lordship's quality is to me much the more agreeable entertainment.

Vaunt-Title: Nay, the world does me the justice to own that no man shows more of the port of a person of quality, or can say more in defence of it against the damned levelling part of the tawn . . .

Enter the **Page.**

Page: Madam, supper's on the table.

Vaunt-Title: Oh Lerd, medem, your ladyship's humble servant. *(Going.)*

Urania: By no means, my lord, if you'll be pleased to share a small collation, you'll do me a peculiar honour. 'Tis a perfect ambign, and word of ceremony, so I beseech your lordship to make none to go to it.

Vaunt-Title: Your ladyship's command, madam, is enough for your humble servant; refuse me . . .

Urania: Come, my Lady Clemene, we'll show the way, and before we part I hope Mr Dorimant and I shall be able to bring you to a more favourable construction of the stage and its friends.

Clemene: Eh! Ged, medem, name not the stage, unless you design to save your supper, for let me say if it be not a perfect vomit to chaste ears!

Witwoud: Madam, when we come to order and method, you shall see me throw this positive knight on his back, or I'll never enter the lists again.

Dorimant: Be not so confident of victory, that often leaves you too open to your adversaries' thrusts. But the town is already almost come off from your court.

> Fancy a while may please the giddy town,
> With that false reasons may a while go down,
> But when at last their fading beauties fail,
> Right reason then and justice will prevail, -
> *End of the First Act*

In Act II, the characters, joined by Hotspur, continue to debate the issues Collier raised in the *Short View* and to mock Collier's ability to see filth where it might or might not exist.

Witwoud: And you don't think the stage really guilty of profaneness?

Hotspur: Less than of immodesty.

Vaunt-Title: Refuse me, thou art a most incorrigible fellow, Jack! *(Laughs.)* I warrant there is no swearing nor cursing on the stage? *(Laughs.)*

Witwoud: Ay, my lord, no swearing. *(Laughs.)*

Clemene: O! Swearing is furiously my aversion, I can't endure the sound of an oath, it makes me start! Let me say, madam, if an oath does not dismantle all the fortifications of my understanding, and leaves my mind for the time a heap of confusion. Why a soldier's oath is as frightful to me as the report of his pistol.

Dorimant: Ah! Madam! What have you said? What shock our ears with so smutty an expression? Modesty is the character of your sex, and to talk out of that is to talk out of character. A soldier's pistol! O hideous!

It is in Act III, however, that Sir Jerry contrives his own revelation as a hypocrite.

Act III

Scene: a garden. Enter Sir Jerry Witwoud and Dorimant.

Dorimant: Thus you see, Sir Jerry that I have made out that the stage is the school of virtue, where vice and folly are exposed, and [. . .] virtue promoted - or to put it into Mr Collier's own words, which are more prevalent with you, I have made it appear that the business of the stage is to recommend virtue, and discountenance vice, to show the uncertainty of humane greatness, the sudden turns of fate, and the unhappy conclusions of violence and injustice, to expose the singularity of pride and fancy, to make folly and falsehood contemptible, and to bring everything that is ill under infamy and neglect.

Witwoud: Go on, sir . . .

Dorimant: Now, Sir Jerry, from this maxim of Mr Collier's, it follows that these vices and these follies must be drawn, or else they could not be exposed. Is it not, therefore an argument of an inveterate hypocrite that makes your reformers such enemies to the stage? If you are such zealots for morality, first reform yourselves. Next, pray, why are you less severe on taverns, brandy shops, and other tippling-houses, on gaming-tables, usurers, oppressors of the poor, betrayers of the public, libellers of the state and church, and the like?

Witwoud: We must do all things by degrees.

Dorimant: You begin therefore with your endeavours to suppress that which from your own confession is useful to [. . .] promoting the end you pretend to, and let those things alone to hereafter which all the world with one voice condemn as pernicious to virtue and to mankind. And let me tell you, Sir Jerry, if the stage did not make its business to expose knaves and hypocrites, you would say nothing to it; 'tis because it declares against you that you are so clamorous against that.

Witwoud: Well, well, Mr Dorimant, let all mankind, reason and demonstration, say what they will, I'm sure I'm in the right . . .

Dorimant: There indeed spoke the enemies of the stage all in one; you are a pleasant arguer, Sir Jerry, on my word.

Witwoud: But you have not touched one thing, the meeting of so many lewd people together.

Dorimant: The same meet at the church, the meeting-house, the park, Epsom, Tonbridge, et cetera.

Witwoud: All, all unlawful meetings, where there are above two or three.

Dorimant: *(Laughs)* But see the ladies . . .

Enter Lord Vaunt-Title, Urania, Eliza and Clemene.

Eliza: My lord, I protest I can gather nothing from all you have said but the very great esteem you have for your own quality.

Vaunt-Title: And don't you think, medem, that others ought to have the like, refuse me! Ha!

Eliza: Refuse you I shall for all that I can discover in your lordship . . .

Clemene: Eh! Ged, medem, you destroy my night's rest by one word more for the stage; it has lost me all the pleasure of this moonlight walk about your charming gardens - Oh, Sir Jerry, I'm sure I come to join in your triumph over this obstinate one.

Dorimant: Faith, madam, we have been like true disputants, both weary, but neither convinced. But I have made a considerable discovery, Madam Clemene, which will shock your esteem for Sir Jerry.

Urania: Ah! Pray let us hear that, Mr Dorimant, for that would be triumph indeed.

Clem: But a triumph, medem, that your ladyship, let me say, will not obtain.

Dorimant: I can assure you that he is now going on a work that will for ever disoblige you.

Clemene: Eh! Ged, Mr Dorimant, that's impossible.

Dorimant: Nay, I confess I may be deceived, and you that could sacrifice your reason to his opinion, may, perhaps, discharge your pleasure and inclination too on that account.

Clemene: That you may be sure of, Mr Dorimant, for, Gad forgive me, I was too too wickedly inclined to see those filthy plays, 'til he and Mr Collier made me a convert . . .

Dorimant: Hear then, madam, thus it is - having deprived you of all rational and honourable recreations, he proceeds to confound your mere diversions too, as Tonbridge, Epsom, the Bath, Richmond, Lambeth and Islington, Wells, High-Park, the Mall, Spring-Garden, nay, the very fields that lead to those wicked places, are to go down; vice and vanity are to be dispatched root and branch, and you must, (as a French Popish prelate has it) like the innocent Jews, divert yourselves with your children at home.

Urania: But what if we have none?

Vaunt-Title: Rat me, medem, you must get 'em. *(Laughing.)* Refuse me if Dorimant be not a pleasant fellow! *(Laughs.)*

Clemene: Eh! Good Mr Dorimant, you kill me - you suffocate me; you put me into insupportable convulsions! - No Epsom! No Tonbridge!

Impossible! It can not be! Speak, Sir Jerry. - Are you so seriously cruel to take away from the ladies our beloved Tonbridge, and all that?

Witwoud: Most certainly, madam; the work of godliness is not to be done by halves! What avails the shutting the doors of that house of Dagon [the god of the Philistines], the playhouse, if we leave him [Dagon] the hills and high places? To drive the devil from his chamber-practice, and leave him the fields?

Clemene: Eh! Ged! But the poor people, let me dee, 'twill be hard on the inhabitants of those places, Sir Jerry, who live by the resort of company.

Witwoud: So do the debauched actors, madam - but for the future let godliness be a gain, and let the wicked starve!

Sir Jerry continues to denounce a variety of social customs, including the lack of respect shown to "ladies of quality" and familiarity between the sexes when "taking the waters" at "the Bath".

Witwoud: Nay, madam, I shall not complement vice, 'tis but one remove from worshipping the devil. I must go on . . .

Clemene: For heaven's sake, sir, consider where you are, and among whom - modesty is the character of our sex; and men that entertain women with rude discourse affront them; (as Mr Collier says) to treat ladies with such stuff, is to presume on their patience to abuse them.

Witwoud: Ay, ay, madam, you may say what you please, but I shall go on! Humility is a virtue, but meanness and sneaking civility to vice is below my character - I must go on, madam . . .

Urania / Eliza: And we'll go off then.

Urania: If these be your stage reformers, deliver us from their doctrine by a speedy conveyance of them to Bedlam . . .

*Exeunt **Urania** and **Eliza**.*

Vaunt-Title: Ha! My pert Eliza slipped away! I'll after her. *(Exit.)*

Clemene: I vow you have frightened away Madam Urania and her cousin but, Sir Jerry, won't you allow the Bath? You know the quality goes there.

Witwoud: I am no respecter of persons. The Bath is the worst of all, for that is like putting men and women to bed together: O Tempora! O Mores!

Clemene: Will you not then allow men and women to meet . . .

Witwoud: No, marry, I won't. What should they meet for? What [. . .] follows the meeting of man and woman? Wickedness, wickedness! Are we not forbid to look on a woman? And can women appear in public without dressing, and showing their faces? Nay, their naked necks and breasts! And then you know how easy the transition is from one part of the naked body to the other. The devil is always at hand, and the flesh always about us. The eyes, the nose, the mouth, and every part, in short, of a pretty woman administers lewd thoughts. If she have a pretty little mouth - why presently men are drawing lewd consequences. By a fine hand and arm, they will be led to a handsome leg and foot, and thence the bars are too feeble to hinder more criminal approaches - and what need is there of all this? Have men entered into a league with wickedness, and are they not content with the ills of solitude, but they must hunt after more in company? Believe me, madam, I know it by experience, all mankind are depraved in their appetites and inclinations; and vice (as Mr Collier proves) is more inviting than virtue. Man was made in solitude. Society was the invention of luxury; and he that built the first city was a murderer. When in the woods the noble savage ran - then there was no whoring, no immorality and prophaneness; no whoring, madam - every man kept his wife or concubine to himself - there was no Epsom, no Tonbridge, no Bath, no Richmond, and the like, to draw whores and rogues together - nay, these places are worse than the playhouses, for there is nothing else to divert them from corrupting men's wives, and spending their money, from gaming, drinking, and all that - but at the play, the wicked play itself may engage them awhile. Then at these places opportunity gives both temptation and relief; at the playhouse some accident may hinder, or at least defer, their wickedness.

Dorimant: Ten to one, Sir Jerry, but that's the reason the ladies have so forsaken the theatre.

Witwoud maintains his attack on those who attend the playhouse, including "the city". During this exchange, Dorimant exits, and Witwoud sums up his case and experience before revealing his passion:

Witwoud: Alas! Madam, we are all mortal - all flesh is frail. And do you think, madam, that any man alive could say so many severe things on both sexes, without having had a sufficient experience of those evils and frailties in himself? And gratitude, joined with these transcendent charms, which your ladyship displays in your resplendent face, are so transporting, and so enthusiastic, that I am borne out of myself, and absolutely forced on what I can't avoid. Oh! Madam, you have raised a passion that cannot be discharged without trouble.

Clemene: What? Not satisfied without a crime.

Witwoud: That I don't know. What is a crime to the wicked, may not be so to the godly. If you guard well the appearance, half the duty of religion is preserved and you avoid the scandal. Now the crime, as to men, is not none, if not known, and in many reputed crimes the scandal is all the offence. Remove that, and the crime vanishes, as particularly in a private amour, where there is no injury . . .

Clemene: Eh! Let me say, if this be not seriously surprising . . .

Witwoud: Or if it were a crime, you look so killing fair, you justify rebellion - and I can no longer waste words where opportunity is so fair. Modesty is the character of your sex, and boldness of mine. Now boldness requires action, and modesty passion - that is, I must attack you and you must not resist - and so the decorum and character of both sexes are preserved. If the poets would bring their lovers to action without so many words, 'twere something - but their fine women often lose their reputation by their coqueting, and might cheaper be happy in deed than in talk - they seem fond of the scandal, and fearful of the pleasure, whereas the pleasure should engage their fondness and the scandal their fear.

Clemene: Admirable doctrine, let me die.

Witwoud: Are you pleased with it, madam? Let me say, (for I will not swear as much as by those bright eyes, or those pretty lips) if I will not immediately reduce it to practice - for till then it is but a useless speculation. *(Offers to kiss and embrace her.)*

Clemene: Let me say, if you are not seriously rude, Sir Jerry . . . Oh! Sir, pray, pray - Egad - what, will you attempt upon my honour?

Witwoud: Not on your honour, madam, only on your person - your honour is only in words, but your pleasure in deeds. Come, come, we are alone, I [am] all over love, and you all over charms!

Clemene: Eh! Lord! Sir Jerry, I swear I'll run away from you.

Witwoud: Come, come you must not strive any longer against your own satisfaction - your honour's safe - put, put off the veil, I know you're a hypocrite.

Clemene: Nay, now you begin to be abusive. I vow I'll call out if you won't let me alone - a hypocrite?

Witwoud: Nay, I'm sure of it, for almost all our party are so.

Clemene: Eh! Let me say, if you be not seriously abusive [. . .] *(To herself.)* He is a charming person - he has wit, nay, and discretion too - and 'tis his interest besides to keep all secret, he knows I find that I am a hypocrite, and, what if I confirm him mine by letting him into the secret, 'twill engage him to celebrate me as a virtuous patroness of his works. Eh! See, Sir

Jerry, I'll call out. Eh! Ged, what are you doing - Sir Jerry - I swear we shall be caught, let me say!

Witwoud: Ay, ay, with pleasure, madam, Gad, if I don't give the formal ladies some encouragement this way, our cause will fall - Oh! My life! My soul! My . . .

Enter the company laughing.

Dorimant: Why, how now, Sir Jerry! What a rape? Bless us, what's become of our Anti-Epsomist? What, is this the effect of solitude?

Urania: What in my garden too? Oh! Hideous! Sir Jerry, I owe something to your quandam gown (for we have heard all) or my footmen and horse-pond should revenge the affront.

Dorimant: But my Lady Clemene - what, will you ever go to the wicked, debauched, lewd, playhouse any more, when the confounder of the stage can so much better divert you?

Clemene: Let me say, my Lady Urania, I'm overjoyed that you came to my rescue - for let me say, what is a weak woman in such a man's hands? But let me die, if Sir Jerry be not a person that of all persons I never took for such a person, but he is become furiously my aversion, and in revenge I will go every day this week to the playhouse . . .

Witwoud: Gentlemen, I am caught - but I hope, since my zeal has been private here, so you'll let my folly be. For if the damned poets should get this story by the end, I shall be worried to death by 'em; I ask your pardon, Lady, and so good night.

Urania: But 'tis fit such a hypocrite should be exposed.

Witwoud: Ah! No. If the hypocrites were exposed, half the town would go naked - and all the stage enemies like me, go off with their tails betwixt their legs.

Exit.

That there is no known riposte by Collier to Brown's play may indicate that he was unaware of it. It seems hard to imagine he would not have responded in some suitably passionate way. Two years later, the Revered Arthur Bedford did respond however. In his *The Evil and Danger of Stage Plays* he describes the plot (a generous word) of *The Stage Beaux* as being "filled with scurrility and profaneness". Meanwhile, the impact the reformers had had on the London scene by 1704 can be assessed from the Epilogue Thomas Brown wrote for the play and which was spoken at the Theatre Royal:

THE STAGE BEAUX TOSS'D IN A BLANKET

Well, gentlemen, this boldly we may say,
However you like it, 'tis a modest play.
There's no prophaneness and no bawdy in't,
 No, not one single double-meaning hint,
And that's enough in so reformed an age,
For all our author to reform the stage.

'Tis now some years since drowsie reformation
Roused its dull head, and saw its restoration
What influence has this had upon the nation?
Ye rakehells of the Rose, let Rouse confess
If at his house he draws one hogshead less.

And you intriguing sparks enquire of Jenny
If it has baulked her of one bawdy guinea!
Is gaming grown a less destructive vice?
Are fewer families undone by dice?
No - for the cunning men the town infest,
 And daily for new quarries are in quest.

Oft times in public they their ends arrive at,
But shoals of bubbles are drawn in in private.
'Tis by these means they furnish out debauches,
And sharpers now like quacks set up their coaches.

Now let us cast our eyes upon the City,
These are no vices - no - none that are witty.
Expensive are the sprightly sins of wits,
But frugal, gainful, vices are for Cits.
They never swear, because for that they pay,
But they will lie - yes - in a trading way.

They've lies in readiness whene'er they barter,
And claim the right of cheating from their charter.
They with suburbian whores ne'er lead their lives.
But why? - why, they can't satisfy their wives.
Besides, with cost the suburb punk they treat,
But they will drink, because e'en drunk they cheat.

Examine all the town, each quarter view,
And we shall find what Butler said is true,
We all are proud for sins we are inclined to,
By damning those we never have a mind to.
Thus reformation has discharged its rage
Upon the vices of the sinking stage.

As ships
When fraught with foreign luxury they sail,
As soon as ever they descry a whale
Throw out a tub to find the monster play,
Lest the rich cargo should become its prey.
So some to turn our furious zealot's rage
From loved high crimes have overthrown the stage.

Gentlemen, briefly this has been our fault,
We more for others than ourselves have thought.
Each man would piously reform his neighbour,
To save himself he thinks not worth his labour.
With zeal and sin at once we're strangely warmed,
And grow more wicked as we grow reformed.

Oh! 'Tis a blessed age, and blessed nation,
When vice walks cheek by jowl with reformation.
In short, let each man's thoughts first look at home,
And then to foreign reformations roam.
If all the fools and knaves met here today,
Would their own faults and follies first survey,
We need not fear their censures of the play.

10

Towards Reform

One Monday night in December 1702, Farquhar's new and savagely satirical comedy *The Twin Rivals* had its first night at the Theatre Royal, Drury Lane. *The Daily Courant* recorded an onstage duel between two members of the audience. *The Flying Post* also reported the incident:

On Monday last Colonel Fielding, commonly called Handsome Fielding, was dangerously wounded in a quarrel with one Mr Goodyear, a gentleman, at the Theatre Royal, Drury Lane.

On the following day, in another theatre-related incident, one Mr Cusaick, "an Irish gentleman", and a Captain Fulwood quarrelled at the New Theatre, Lincoln's Inn Fields and afterwards fought. Mr Cusaick was seriously wounded, but Captain Fulwood was killed on the spot and was "very decently" buried the following Sunday evening at St Clement Dane's in the Strand. The stage was still a lively place - so to speak.

But that year had also seen the accession to the throne of Queen Anne - the daughter of James II. She was not perhaps the wisest of women and was easily influenced by those around her. Maybe for the latter reason, maybe because she was indeed aware of the changing times, she made a number of attempts to regulate the playhouses. Soon after acceding, she issued a proclamation which, after desiring that

149

"nothing might be acted contrary to religion and good manners", decreed that "no person of what quality soever should go behind the scenes or come upon the stage whether before or during the acting of any play". The decree was repeated in different forms at decent intervals - and ignored. Queen Anne and her Court officials were finding it difficult to gain any power over the stage. As we have seen, however, there were occasions when individual actors were prosecuted for speaking the name of God on stage and, in one case, for uttering speeches in *The Provoked Wife* such as the lines about "cowardly company, fellows that went to church and said grace to their meat and had not the least tincture of quality about them".

Queen Anne had inherited a situation (see Chapter Two) in which her Master of Revels was censor only by tradition - a tradition which, furthermore, had fallen into abeyance. Convention was therefore a major obstacle to reform. It could also be legally argued (and was argued) that plays licensed in the "looser" days of King Charles II and James II had a continuing right be performed.

One of the Queen's next attempts to exert control was made through the Lord Chamberlain. A 1704 proclamation records a complaint that "old as well as new plays are still acted without due care to leave out such expressions as are contrary to religion and good manners". In this document, the Lord Chamberlain went on to complain that the acting companies "got up" plays without sending them to the Master of Revels and especially that "prologues, epilogues and songs which are often indecent are brought upon the stage without his licence". "Fair copies" of new plays, prologues, epilogues and songs therefore had to be sent to the Master of the Revels. Furthermore, the Lord Chamberlain now insisted that the players "do not presume to act upon the stage any play, new or old, containing profane or indecent expressions" and commanded the Master of Revels to "read diligently" plays submitted to him.

Few records of the censoring activities of the Master of Revels exist from this period. In 1706, Farquhar had to clean up the printed version of *The Recruiting Officer* between its first and second editions. The prompt copies of two plays by the little known Charles Johnson, dating from 1710, show that passages which could be judged irreligious or lacking respect for the clergy were censored. It can also be deduced from publications such as the playwright Colley Cibber's *An Apology for His Life* that censorship had become stricter. However, this intermittent censorship was still based on tradition rather than law and Cibber, for one, regularly defied the Court officials. The critics of the stage, including Collier (see Chapter Eight) still had their work cut out.

On the first Sunday of January 1705, the Reverend Arthur Bedford launched himself into the controversy as an advocate of stage reform. His sermon that Sunday was subsequently published as *Serious Reflections on the Scandalous Abuse and Effects of the Stage: in a Sermon Preached at the Parish Church of St Nicholas in the City of Bristol.* Later that year he was to publish *A Second Advertisement Concerning the Prophaneness of the Playhouse*, to be followed in 1706 by a more extended attack.

Just as Collier had been a disciple of Rymer, so Arthur Bedford was of Collier. He had taken his MA at Brazenose College in 1691, and was ordained soon afterwards. He became chaplain to the Duke of Bedford and remained largely out of contact with the secular, everyday world. Nevertheless, he considered himself to be a proper guardian of the public morals. He, too, was a non-juring priest. Between 1704 and 1719, he published many attacks on the stage and music, equating them with "the devil and all his works, the pomps and vanities of this wicked world". That first published sermon was prompted by the building of a theatre in the nearby city of Bath. In his sermon, he first quotes the Epistle of Paul to Timothy: "Shun profane and vain babblings for they will increase into more ungodliness." He then quotes Collier's *Short View* as "proof sufficient that playhouse diversions are 'vain babblings'". When the spa baths at Bath ran dry and so lost their healing powers, he pointed out that a company of touring players was performing in the city.

His 1706 publication had as its splendidly precise, if less than snappy, title *The Evil and Danger of Stage Plays: Showing their Natural Tendency to Destroy Religion and Introduce a Grand Corruption of Manners; in Almost Two Thousand Instances, Taken from the Plays of the Two Last Years, against All the Methods Lately Used for Their Reformation.* It is indeed, by and large, a catalogue of some 2,000 instances of swearing, blasphemy, and profanity. When a character is censured for swearing,

Bedford provides some thirty scriptural texts denouncing swearing. Many of these 2,000 instances are from Tom Brown's attack on Collier. Bedford also finds many unacceptable details in Farquhar's *The Recruiting Officer*:

> One captain is represented as a notorious liar, another as a drunkard, one intrigues with women, another is scandalously guilty of debauching them.

In all this single-mindedness, Bedford was not without some self-awareness. He recognises that he is attacking writers who are acknowledged as men of "wit and ingenuity" and admits that his attack exposes himself to ridicule. This did not deter him. By 1719, he followed up this catalogue with a sequel. *A Serious Remonstrance* contained some 7,000 further instances. It should be noted that, in all this stunningly pedantic work, he had the whole-hearted approval of men such as Defoe.

There were critical defences of the stage during the reign of Queen Anne - though many were anonymous. One of the signed ones was a 1702 letter addressed "To the Honourable George Granville, Esquire" by John Dennis. In it, he provides a useful commentary on changing public tastes, even if passages sound somewhat élitist:

> But Sir, whether the general taste of England ever was good or no, this I think cannot be controverted, that the taste of England for comedy ... was certainly much better in the reign of King Charles the Second than it is at present ...
>
> First then, in the reign of King Charles the Second, a considerable part of an audience had those parts which were requisite for the judging of comedy ... principally a fine imagination and a sound judgement ...
>
> Secondly then, in the reign of King Charles the Second, a considerable part of an audience had such an education as qualified them to judge of comedy. That reign was a reign of pleasure. Even the entertainments of their closet were all delightful. Poetry and eloquence were then their studies and that human, gay and sprightly philosophy which qualified them to relish the only reasonable pleasures which man can have in the world, and those are conversation and dramatic poetry ... All the sheer originals in town were known and in some measure copied. But now the case is vastly different. For all those great and numerous originals are reduced to one single coxcomb, and that is the foolish false politician.

For from Westminster to Wapping, go where you will, the conversation turns upon politics . . .

Besides, there are three sorts of people now in our audiences who have had no education at all and who were unheard of in the reign of King Charles the Second. A great many younger brothers, gentlemen born, who have been kept at home, by reason of the pressure of the taxes. Several people who made their fortunes in the late war and who, from a state of obscurity and perhaps of misery, have risen to a condition of distinction and plenty . . .

But thirdly, in the reign of King Charles the Second, a considerable part of an audience had that due application, which is requisite for the judging of comedy. They had first of all leisure to attend to it. For that was an age of pleasure and not of business. They were serene enough to receive its impressions, for they were in ease and plenty. But in the present reign, a great part of the gentlemen have not leisure, because want throws them upon employments and there are ten times more gentlemen now in business than there were in King Charles's reign. Nor have they serenity . . . by reason that they are attentive to the events of affairs and too full of great and real events to receive due impressions from the imaginary ones of the theatre. They come to a playhouse full of some business which they have been soliciting, or of some harangue which they are to make the next day, so that they merely come to unbend and are utterly incapable of duly attending to the just and harmonious symmetry of a beautiful design.

Or, as Professor Krutch puts it, with greater hindsight and from a different stance:

The orgy of dissipation into which the ruling class plunged after the Restoration could not possibly last . . . As the effects of the reaction passed, English moderation naturally reasserted itself.

Dennis continued to defend the stage from, among other things, opera. In 1706, he published his *Essay on the Operas after the Italian Manner* in which he argued that, as official disapproval of plays continued to mount, operas threatened to drive straight plays and comedies from the stage. Hence his desire:

. . . to defend the English stage, which together with our English liberties has descended to us from our ancestors; to defend it against that deluge of mortal foes which have come pouring in from the continent to drive out the muses, its old inhabitants, and seat themselves in their stead.

His lament has a neat modern parallel with those who complain that London's theatres are dominated by American musicals.

Dennis was to maintain his defence of the stage until 1726 when he published his fourth and last work on the subject, *The Stage Defended*. This work can fairly be described as the final contemporary contribution to the Jeremy Collier Controversy. It was a reply to yet another non-juror, William Law, who had published in the same year his 50-page argument, *The Absolute Unlawfulness of the Stage-Entertainment Fully Demonstrated*. This is significant because it was the last attack in Collier's lifetime and because of the response it provoked from Dennis. Law's point was not that the stage encouraged sin but that it was intrinsically wicked:

> It is condemned as drunkenness and lewdness, as lying and prophaneness are to be condemned; not as things that may only be the occasions of sin but as such are in their own nature grossly sinful.

For Law, the stage was as sinful as the worship of images. Full stop. As well as provoking Dennis into a reply, it also resulted in an eight-page piece of invective by one who signed herself Mrs S____ O____. This unknown author, one of the very few women to enter the debate, damns Law for presuming "publicly to libel and defame my favourite diversion". The title of her pamphlet neatly summarises its content: *A Short Reply to Mr Law's Long Declamation against the Stage. Wherein the Wild Rant, Blind Passion and False Reasoning of that Piping-hot Pharisee are Made Apparent to the Meanest Capacity*. Dennis's answer was more measured.

He defends comedy and tragedy as "the only genuine legitimate entertainments of the stage". He refutes Law's assertions, quoting St Paul, Molière, Milton, an archbishop and several classical authors. He emphasises that plays have not encouraged swearing and profanity but that their recent suppression has in fact encouraged gambling, maintaining that "gaming has increased ten-fold since Collier's books were published". He repeatedly points out that the attacks on the stage have come from non-juring, and therefore suspect, priests:

> For what is Mr Law? And what are his predecessors, Collier and Bedford who attacked the stage before him? Why, Jacobite non-juring parsons, all three of them, who have disowned our established church and disowned our Government.

Two other contributions to the later stages of the debate deserve some notice. One was from a lawyer, Edward Filmer, thought to be a possible author of earlier, anonymous pamphlets. In 1707 he published *A Defence of Plays: or The Stage Vindicated*. From his preface, it is clear that he admired Collier's learning and skill and even admits to respecting Collier's wit. He also stands alongside Collier in maintaining that there were abuses in the drama and then criticises the tactics of the playwrights in defending only their own plays and not the stage itself:

> Whilst everyone flew to the defence of his own particular concern, the stage was left naked, exposed to all the most furious assaults of a violent and implacable enemy.

Filmer uses the structure of the *Short View* for his *Defence*, refuting Collier's arguments chapter by chapter. It has to be said that the *Defence* is verbose and few new points are made. His main thrust, lawyer that he is, is that plays should be regulated on the principle of poetic justice. The stage should not be reformed, as Collier sometimes maintained, by the removal of bad characters but by ensuring "a constant proportionate reward of virtue and punishment of vice". He therefore suggests that smut is not dangerous in itself, provided it is put in the mouth of a "vicious" (and punished) character. He also suggests that, if a play is to condemn human failings, it must show them. And, as he very reasonably points out, if nothing happens on stage that might not happen in a drawing room, you would have no drama.

We may now feel that, were all plays to end on a note of poetic justice, we should have only the blandest of drama. Nevertheless, Filmer's view became increasingly popular and was taken up by many, including the essayist Steele. It explains, incidentally, why Nahum Tate's adaptation of *King Lear*, in which the wronged Cordelia does not die but lives happily ever after, was more popular than Shakespeare's play throughout the eighteenth century.

But Filmer's dull compromise was not universally popular. It provoked Collier himself to return to the argument and in 1708 he published his final contribution to the debate, *A Farther Vindication of the Short View of the Profaneness and Immorality of the English Stage; in Which the Objections of a Late Book Entitled* A Defence of Plays *are Considered*. It is written with savage and sarcastic anger, as he dissects

Filmer phrase by phrase, again quoting classical authors as his evidence:

> He lays it down for a maxim that if smut and profaneness can't be allowed, the poets must have few or no characters to practise on. These things it seems are necessary ingredients of diversion and fundamental to the satisfaction of mankind. But then, to varnish over the matter, he tells us, 'Smut must not be out of character or too gross in terms or sense; but when 'tis wrapped up in clean linen and lies in double entendres, 'tis easy and natural' - and he sees no great danger in it. It may be so. However, Livy was not at all of the Doctor's [Filmer's] mind.

Collier frequently refers Filmer to his (Collier's) earlier statements and concludes that a defence of the playhouse is impractical and that ribaldry and prophaneness will never be acceptable in a Christian country. Otherwise, it must be said that the *Farther Vindication* is little more than a repetition of Collier's earlier arguments.

The ten years that followed its appearance were relatively calm ones so far as the controversy was concerned. D'Urfey offered a couple of side-swipes at Collier in the Prologue and Epilogue to his 1709 play *The Old Mode and the New*. In the Prologue, he taunts Collier for not maintaining his attack but for busying himself with his *Historical Dictionary* of which D'Urfey has a low opinion:

> Our late absolving saint new broached this trade:
> He that late, huge, false Dictionary made,
> And left reforming to be better paid.

But by the time he reaches his Epilogue, D'Urfey is again taking Collier seriously:

> Don't swear nor say 'a pox', for he'll inform.
> He hates all oaths and such rude blustering folly,
> But cants and lies like any side-box molly.

The side-box of a theatre was a favourite seat of the more exhibitionist members of the audience. The word "molly" was in colloquial use at this time to mean an effeminate homosexual but was also used, at least once by D'Urfey, to mean a prostitute.

In 1717, Colley Cibber mounted a major attack on Collier in his play *The Non-juror* which depicts "an English popish priest lurking under the doctrine of our own church to raise his own fortune". It was a clever device by Cibber to gain him the approval of the new King,

George I, and popularity with the public. It worked. The King rewarded Cibber with £200 and the poet laureateship; the play ran for eighteen days running which was a rare long run for the period. It did provoke antagonistic reactions however.

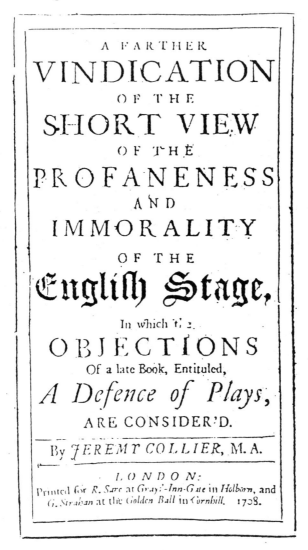

A FARTHER
VINDICATION
OF THE
SHORT VIEW
OF THE
PROFANENESS
AND
IMMORALITY
OF THE
𝕰𝖓𝖌𝖑𝖎𝖘𝖍 𝕾𝖙𝖆𝖌𝖊,
In which t' .
OBJECTIONS
Of a late Book, Entituled,
A Defence of Plays,
ARE CONSIDER'D.

By *JEREMY COLLIER*, M.A.

LONDON:
Printed for *R. Sare* at *Gray's-Inn-Gate* in *Holborn*, and *G. Strahan* at the *Golden Ball* in *Cornhill.* 1708.

Figure 9: *A Farther Vindication of the* Short View

The most caustic was a pamphlet called *The Theatre Royal Turned into a Mountebank's Stage*, stated to be "by a non-juror". Sister Rose Anthony suggests its author was in fact Collier and lists eight similarities of phrasing between it and Collier's other works. For example, the playhouse is called "a nursery of vice and debauchery" in both *The Theatre Royal Turned* and in the *Short View*. That might equally be coincidence or plagiarism. It certainly seems odd if Collier did not respond and he would have had good reasons to do so anonymously because, since the Jacobite rebellion of 1715 in favour of the deposed King James, Jacobites had been prohibited from publishing their views. But the play is about non-jurors, not stage reform, and so is outside the scope of this book.

Bedford, Dennis and Law, as well as a number of anonymous writers, were to make their last contributions to the debate during the following decade, but by now the Jeremy Collier Controversy had run its course.

The victory of the reformers was slow and, so far, partial. Indeed, they had signally failed to bring about any change in the law. What they had changed was public opinion. The playwrights and theatre managers had therefore begun to regulate themselves, in order to maintain the theatre's popularity. As we have said, the Master of the Revels was beginning to make attempts at censorship; but at no time in the period we have been discussing did the Crown succeed in gaining the legal powers over the theatres that it wanted. George I faced the same problems as had Anne. Soon after his accession in 1714, he issued a licence for the proper management of 'his' theatre, the Theatre Royal in Drury Lane:

> ... by our royal licence bearing the date the 18th day of October 1714, we did give and grant unto Richard Steele Esq., now Sir Richard Steele, Knight, Mr Robert Wilks, Mr Colley Cibber, Mr Thomas Doggett and Mr Barton Booth, full power, licence and authority to form, constitute and establish for us a company of comedians with free licence to act and represent comedies, tragedies and other theatrical performances, subject to such rules and orders for the good government therein as they shall receive from time to time from the Chamberlain of our Household, such licence to continue during our pleasure and no longer.

But, as Cibber pointed out in his *Apology*, this loosely worded document "made us sole judges of what plays might be proper for the stage without submitting them to the approbation or licence of any other particular person". Cibber had earlier suffered from Killigrew's interventions when the latter had censored the entire first act of *Richard III* on the grounds that it would remind people of James II, then still living over the water in France. Cibber had asked for selective cuts. Impossible said Killigrew: he hadn't the leisure to consider which details might be offensive. So now Cibber was in a position to get his own back. Soon after George I's document came into force, a new play needed licensing. The Master of Revels, Charles Killigrew, now an elderly man, asked for his usual fee. Cibber popped round to see him, told him he had no authority over the theatre and refused to pay him any more fees. The power of the Master of the Revels was effectively over.

Perhaps not surprisingly, petitions were got up and sent to various Court officials claiming that "the use of the theatre has for many years been much perverted to the great scandal of religion and good government". By October 1718, a letter had reached the Attorney General stating that the Drury Lane management was refusing to obey the orders and regulations of the Lord Chamberlain who still, of course, had no legal powers of censorship.

The King did have one weapon. "Having received information of great misbehaviours committed by our company of comedians now acting at the theatre in Drury Lane," and for "neglect of a due subordination and submission to the authority of our Chamberlain and other officers of our household," he revoked their licence. This revocation was dated January 23rd and has been ascribed by various commentators to both the years 1719 and 1720. This is another example of confusion resulting from use of the old and new style calendars. At this period, the new year still began in March - so although the revocation appears to us to be dated January 23rd 1720, it actually appeared towards the end of 1719. Even this episode ended unsatisfactorily from the Court's viewpoint, with Cibber and Steele being reinstated within two years.

Few attempts at censorship seem to have been made during the 1720s. This was partly due to the rise of "sentimental comedy" -

popularised largely by Steele in response to the demands of the public and critics. Typically, a sentimental comedy did not present any low characters on stage but featured "good and exceedingly generous" ones. They included scenes designed to provoke tears as much as laughter with virtuous behaviour rewarded and vices such as drinking and duelling condemned. Not surprisingly, they lacked realism and dramatic interest. One of Steele's own sentimental comedies, *The Conscious Lovers* (1722), is typical of the genre and has been described as "one of the worst examples of a moral play devoid of the comic spirit". If Collier and his supporters had turned a brilliant but immoral tradition into a dull and moral one, Goldsmith and Sheridan would revive the best and wittiest aspects of Restoration comedy later in the century.

Meanwhile, the number of London theatres was increasing and consequently so was competition for audiences. This was also a period of some distinctly lively journalism as more and more newspapers were founded. The Government became a popular target for the new breed of political satirists, who included Addison and Swift. Not surprisingly, political satire spread to the stage. One work in particular proved consistently popular: John Gay's *The Beggar's Opera*. Although it attacked the great and the good in very general terms, audiences had no trouble in seeing references to members of George II's Court and Prime Minister Walpole's Cabinet. Walpole, apparently, sat with a fixed, forced smile on his face for the duration of its first night performance. When Gay wrote a sequel, *Polly*, the following year, Walpole had a word with his friend, the Duke of Grafton who was the Lord Chancellor. *Polly* was banned from the stage, although it did appear in print.

Three years later, Henry Fielding had his first stage success, at the Little Theatre, Haymarket which was an unlicensed and therefore technically illegal theatre. His subsequent plays proved even more popular and in 1731 *The Welsh Opera* attacked Walpole's public and private morals quite openly. It portrayed the King and Queen as the hen-pecked Squire and the voluble Lady Ap-Shinkin, while Walpole became their light-fingered butler. Walpole gave Fielding an official warning. *The Welsh Opera* was revised as *The Grub Street Opera* but had no known staging until 1993. The next major event in the story happened in 1736 when Fielding took over the Haymarket Theatre. He opened with a social and political satire, *Pasquin*. Audiences delighted in its topical darts and jibes and it ran for nearly seventy performances - an amazing achievement for the period. And nothing was said, officially.

But Walpole was in trouble. His power base was slipping and he was no longer the royal favourite. Then in the next February, Fielding presented *The Historical Register for the Year 1736*. London had no doubt that its central character, the fiddler Quidam who bribes people to dance to his tunes, was Walpole.

Walpole decided it was "time to protect" the public. He introduced a seemingly innocent Bill in Parliament "to explain and amend" an Act dating from Queen Anne's time exerting control over "rogues, vagabonds, sturdy beggars and vagrants". Under Walpole's new Bill, actors performing in places where they had no licence so to do would be "deemed rogues and vagabonds". Only two theatres were to be licensed: the two royal patent houses - Drury Lane and Covent Garden. Consequently, no theatrical performances would be allowed outside London. New plays and additions to old ones would require the permission of the Lord Chamberlain. Failure to comply would mean a fine of £50 and the loss of the theatre's licence. The Lord Chamberlain was to have the power to proscribe plays "as often as he shall think fit" and to close any theatre he fancied.

The Bill faced considerable opposition in Parliament. Most notably, it elicited a famous speech from Lord Chesterfield, a speech which still sums up the case against censorship:

> My Lords: The Bill now before you I apprehend to be of a very extraordinary, a very dangerous nature. It seems designed not only as a restraint on the licentiousness of the stage; but it will prove a most arbitrary restraint on the liberty of the stage. And I fear it looks yet further. I fear it tends towards a restraint on the liberty of the press, which will be a long stride towards the destruction of liberty itself . . .

This particular fear was to prove unfounded, but Chesterfield rightly pointed out the danger of accepting the principle of censorship:

> I am as much for restraining the licentiousness of the stage, and every sort of licentiousness, as any of your lordships can be. But, my Lords, I

am, I shall always be, extremely cautious and fearful of making the least encroachment upon liberty.

Chesterfield also revealed himself to have a good understanding of popular taste:

By this Bill you prevent a play's being acted but you do not prevent its being printed; therefore, if a licence should be refused for its being acted, we may depend upon it the play will be printed. It will be printed and published, my lords, with the refusal in capital letters upon the title page. People are always fond of what is forbidden.

He moved on to give his definition of the purpose of the stage:

My Lords, the proper business of the stage and that for which only it is useful, is to expose those vices and follies which the laws cannot lay hold of; and to recommend those beauties and virtues which ministers and courtiers seldom either imitate or reward. But by laying it under a licence, and under an arbitrary court licence too, you will, in my opinion, entirely pervert its use. For though I have the greatest esteem for that noble duke, in whose hands this power is at present designed to fall, though I have an entire confidence in his judgement and impartiality, yet I may suppose that a leaning towards the fashions of a Court is sometimes hard to be avoided.

He came to this ringing conclusion:

If poets and players are to be restrained, let them be restrained as other subjects are, by the known laws of their country. If they offend, let them be tried, as every Englishman ought to be, by God and their country. Do not let us subject them to the arbitrary will and pleasure of any one man. A power lodged in the hands of one single man to judge and determine, without any limitation, without any control or appeal, is a sort of power unknown to our laws, inconsistent with our constitution. It is a higher, more absolute power than we trust even to the King himself; and therefore I think we ought not invest any such power in His Majesty's Lord Chamberlain.

But they did. The Bill was passed. Among the provisions of the new 1737 Licensing Act were the following clauses:

Every person who shall, for hire, gain or reward, act, represent or perform, or cause to be acted, represented or performed any interlude, tragedy, comedy, opera, play, farce or other entertainment of the stage, or any part or parts therein, in case such person shall not have any legal settlement in the place where the same shall be acted, represented or performed without authority by virtue of letters patent from His Majesty, his heirs, successors or predecessors, or without licence from the Lord Chamberlain of His Majesty's household for the time being, shall be deemed to be a rogue and a vagabond within the intent and meaning of the said recited Act, and shall be liable and subject to all such penalties and punishments, and by such methods of conviction as are inflicted on or appointed by the said Act for the punishment of rogues and vagabonds who shall be found wandering, begging and misordering themselves, within the intent and meaning of the said recited Act.

No new play could now be performed:

. . . unless a true copy thereof be sent to the Lord Chamberlain of the King's household for the time being, fourteen days at least before the acting, representing or performing thereof, together with an account of the playhouse or other place where the same shall be and the time when the same is intended to be first acted, represented or performed, signed by the master or manager, or one of the masters or managers of such playhouse or place, or company of actors therein.

And, of course, the Lord Chamberlain could:

. . . prohibit the acting, performing or representing any interlude, tragedy, comedy, opera, play, farce or other entertainment of the stage, or any act, scene or part thereof, or any prologue or epilogue.

A Licenser of Stage Plays, William Chetwynd, was appointed at an annual salary of £400. His deputy or Examiner, at half the salary, was Thomas Odell, the founder of the Goodman's Fields Theatre. All new plays, adaptations or additions to old plays, prologues and epilogues now had to be submitted by the managers of the two licensed theatres to the Lord Chamberlain for examination at least fourteen days before they were intended to be performed. Only if approved and after any required cuts had been made would he grant a licence to perform.

Stage censorship had come about for political reasons but the law was quickly used to censor profanity and immorality. Indirectly and posthumously, Collier had won.

163

Conclusion

"A Stuart toy, walled off from the life of the nation as a whole, mirroring the tastes of the King and his Court." This description of Restoration comedy from Richard Findlater's review of theatrical censorship, *Banned!*, encapsulates the paradox of the form. It is both realistic and escapist. It realistically reflects the daily life, the interests and preoccupations of a narrow segment of a privileged society. It is realistic, too, in that it reflects increasing tensions between a liberal aristocracy and an increasingly powerful Puritan middle class.

But it is escapist in that money and amatory problems are always solved to the satisfaction of the young and the gallant. Illness, pain and poverty are never lasting problems for its heroes and heroines. It is also significant that its supporters rarely attempted to deny the presence of "immorality and prophaneness" in Restoration comedy. By and large, they admitted its license and merely attempted to justify it, not disprove it. To its admirers it was, and is, scintillating, dazzling and fun.

To those trying to earn a living outside this "walled garden" for pleasure-seeking fops, that was simply not enough. To the puritan outsider, it seemed a world of libertines rather than liberals; a world of decadence and dissipation.

If one begins with Collier's assumption that pleasure is intrinsically evil, drama, and especially comedy, is automatically suspect. Unable to accept its purpose, Collier could not appreciate that the theatre might be simply a place of entertainment. To write about something he did not understand was to invite ridicule. And since his subject was comedy and a sense of humour was not his strong point, it was doubly inevitable that many saw him as a comic character - especially as he overstated his case and saw filth where there was none. No wonder he was attacked as an interfering busy-body, a spoilsport and as being destructive. But he was also intelligent and extraordinarily well read. He could be sarcastically witty and devastating in debate. And if he failed to realise that pleasure could be an end in itself, he did realise that a play needs to be interesting; a point some of his followers were to forget.

His ultimate object may have been to abolish the stage. In much of his writing he, possibly pragmatically, contented himself with arguing for its reform. His opponents exploited this inconsistency - as they did the fact that he, a traditionalist, rejected the established church. Even so, he got what he wanted. For all his pomposity, for all his over-statements, he was not ineffectual. He was largely responsible for ending Congreve and Vanbrugh's careers as dramatists. But he was not a sole crusader who changed the course of literary history.

Collier's writings reflect the changing climate of society, the changing intellectual mood. He wrote at the dawn of the Augustan age with its increasing emphasis on judgement over fancy, and on morality over libertinism. Like the leader writer of a modern, right-wing tabloid newspaper, he formulated unspoken opinions and successfully articulated the widespread views of, in his case, the middle-classes. It can be argued that he merely led people where they were going anyway, but he certainly speeded up the journey. Restoration comedy would have eventually died. Collier precipitated its demise. More tellingly, he helped create an atmosphere in which censorship would seem acceptable.

In his "Life of Congreve" in *The Lives of the Poets*, Doctor Johnson refers to the Collier controversy. It is hard to better his summary of Collier's purpose, limitations and achievements:

About this time began the long-continued controversy between Collier and the poets. In the reign of Charles the First, the Puritans had raised a violent clamour against the drama, which they considered as an entertainment not lawful to Christians, an opinion held by them in common with the church of Rome . . . The outrages and crimes of the Puritans brought afterwards their whole system of doctrine into disrepute, and from the Restoration the poets and players were left at quiet; for to have molested them would have had the appearance of tendency to puritanical malignity.

This danger, however, was worn away by time; and Collier, a fierce and implacable Non-juror, knew that an attack upon the theatre would never make him suspected for a Puritan. He therefore (1698) published *A Short View of the Immorality and Profaneness of the English Stage*, I believe with no other motive than religious zeal and honest indignation. He was formed for a controvertist; with sufficient learning; with diction vehement and pointed, though often vulgar and incorrect; with unconquerable pertinacity; with wit in the highest degree keen and sarcastic; and with all those powers exalted and invigorated by just confidence in his cause.

Thus qualified, and thus incited, he walked out to battle, and assailed at once most of the living writers, from Dryden to D'Urfey. His onset was violent. Those passages which, while they stood single had passed with little notice, when they were accumulated and exposed together, excited horror; the wise and the pious caught the alarm, and the nation wondered why it had so long suffered irreligion and licentiousness to be openly taught at the public charge.

Nothing now remained for the poets but to resist or fly. Dryden's conscience, or his prudence, angry as he was, withheld him from the conflict; Congreve and Vanbrugh attempted answers. Congreve, a very young man, elated with success, and impatient of censure, assumed an air of confidence and security. His chief artifice of controversy is to retort upon his adversary his own words: he is very angry, and, hoping to conquer Collier with his own weapons, allows himself in the use of every term of contumely and contempt . . . Collier replied; for contest was his delight, he was not to be frighted from his purpose or his prey . . .

The stage found other advocates, and the dispute was protracted through ten years; but at last comedy grew more modest, and Collier lived to see the reward of his labour in the reformation of the theatre.

Bibliography

Jeremy Collier's Works

The Desertion [of James II] *Discussed in a Letter to a Country Gentleman.* 1688.

A volume of essays, including *Upon the Office of a Chaplain.* 1697.

A Short View of the Immorality and Profaneness of the English Stage; 1698 (Three editions), 1699; translated into French, 1715.

A Defence of the Short View of the Profaneness and Immorality of the English Stage *etc: Being a Reply to Mr Congreve's* Amendments *etc and to* The Vindication of the Author of The Relapse. 1699.

A Second Defence of the Short View of the Profaneness and Immorality of the English Stage *etc: Being a Reply to a Book Entitled* The Ancient and Modern Stages Surveyed *etc.* 1700.

Historical Dictionary. Vol. I, II. 1701.

Mr Collier's Dissuasive from the Playhouse, in a Letter to a Person of Quality Occasioned by the Late Calamity of the Tempest. 1703, 1704.

Historical Dictionary. Supplement & Appendix. 1705.

A Farther Vindication of the Short View of the Profaneness and Immorality of the English Stage, *in Which the Objections of a Late Book Entitled* A Defence of Plays *are Considered.* 1708.

Ecclesiastical History of Great Britain. Vol. I, II. 1714.

Reasons for Restoring Some Prayers & Directions as They Stand in the Communion Service of the First English Reformed Liturgy. 1717.

Editor & Compiler of the *Revised Prayer Book.* (Unauthorized) 1718.

A Short View of the Profaneness and Immorality of the English Stage etc, with the Several Defences of the Same. 1730, 1738.

The Jeremy Collier Controversy: A Selective and Chronological List

Including, in sequence, Collier's own responses

Gildon, Charles. *Phaeton: or the Fatal Divorce. A Tragedy: With Some Reflections on a Book Called* A Short View of the Immorality and Profaneness of the English Stage. 1698.

Dryden, John. *Poetical Epistle to Peter Motteux on His Tragedy called* Beauty in Distress. 1698.

Anonymous. *A Letter to A H Esq.; Concerning the Stage.* 1698.

Anonymous. *A Defence of Dramatic Poetry. Being a Review of Mr Collier's View of the Immorality and Profaneness of the Stage.* 1698.

Dennis, John. *The Usefulness of the Stage, to the Happiness of Mankind, to Government and to Religion. Occasioned by a Late Book, written by Jeremy Collier, MA.* 1698.

D'Urfey, Thomas. *The Campaigners, With a Familiar Preface Upon a Late Reformer of the Stage.* 1698.

Vanbrugh, Sir John. *A Short Vindication of* The Relapse *and* The Provoked Wife, *from Immorality and Profaneness.* 1698.

Congreve, William. *Amendments of Mr Collier's False and Imperfect Citations etc. From* The Old Bachelor, Double Dealer, Love for Love, Mourning Bride. *By the Author of those Plays.* 1698.

Anonymous. *AnimadVersions on Mr Congreve's Late Answer to Mr Collier, in a Dialogue between Mr Smith and Mr Johnson. With the Characters of the Present Poets and Some Offers towards New-Modelling the Stage.* 1698.

Anonymous (Ridpath, George?). *The Stage Condemned, and the Encouragement Given to the Immoralities and Profaneness of the Theatre, by the English Schools, Universities and Pulpits, Censured. King Charles I. Sundays Mask and Declaration for Sports and Pastimes on the Sabbath, Largely Related and Animadverted upon. The Arguments of All the Authors that*

BIBLIOGRAPHY

Have Writ in Defence of the Stage Against Mr Collier, Considered. And the Sense of the Fathers, Councils, Antient Philosophers and Poets, and of the Greek and Roman States, and of the First Christian Emperors Concerning the Drama, Faithfully Delivered. Together with The Censure of the English State and of Several Antient and Modern Divines of the Church of England Upon the Stage and Remarks on Diverse Late Plays, as Also on Those Presented by the Two Universities to King Charles I. 1698

Anonymous. *The Immorality of the English Pulpit, as Justly Subjected to the Notice of the English Stage, as the Immorality of the Stage is to That of the Pulpit. In a Letter to Mr Collier Occasioned by the Third Chapter of his Book, Entitled* A Short View of the Immorality of the English Stage. 1698

Collier, Jeremy. *A Defence of the* Short View of the Profaneness and Immorality of the English Stage, *etc. Being a Reply to Mr Congreve's Amendments, etc. And to the* Vindication of the Author of The Relapse. *1699*

Anonymous. *The Stage Acquitted. Being a Full Answer to Mr Collier and the Other Enemies of the Drama, With a Vindication of King Charles the Martyr and the Clergy of the Church of England, from the Abuses of a Scurrilous Book Called* The Stage Condemned. *To Which is Added the Character of the Animadverter, and the Animadversions on Mr Congreve's* Answer to Mr Collier. 1699.

Anonymous (Drake, James?). *The Antient and Modern Stages Surveyed: Or, Mr Collier's View of the Immorality and Profaneness of the English Stage Set in True Light. Wherein Some of Mr Collier's Mistakes are Rectified, and the Comparative Morality of the English Stage is Asserted Upon the Parallel.* 1699.

Dryden, John. "*To Mrs Elizabeth Thomas, Jun.*" Dated November, 1699. Letter XLII, *The Works of John Dryden*, edited by Sir Walter Scott, revised Saintsbury. 1885.

Collier, Jeremy. *A Second Defence of the* Short View of the Prophaneness and Immorality of the English Stage, *etc. Being a Reply to a Book Entitled,* The Ancient and Modern Stages Surveyed, *etc.* 1700.

Cibber, Colley. *Love Makes a Man.* 1700.

Dryden, John. "*Preface Prefixed to* The Fables", 1700. In *The Works of John Dryden*, edited by Sir Walter Scott, revised Saintsbury. 1885

Dryden, John. "*Epilogue to* The Pilgrim", 1700. In *The Dramatic Works of John Dryden.*

Dennis, John. *Letter to the Hon. George Glanville*. 1702.

Collier, Jeremy. *A Dissuasive from the Playhouse; In a Letter to a Person of Quality. Occasioned by the Late Calamity of the Tempest*. 1703

Anonymous (Woodward, Josiah). *Some Thoughts Concerning the Stage in a Letter to a Lady*. 1704.

Dennis, John. *The Person of Quality's Answer to Mr Collier's Letter Containing a Defence of a Regulated Stage*, 1704.

Brown, Thomas. *The Stage-Beaux Toss'd in a Blanket; Or, Hypocrisie . . . à la Mode; Exposed in a True Picture of Jerry . . . A Pretending Scourge to the English Stage: A Comedy. With a Prologue on Occasional Conformity; and an Epilogue on the Reformers*. 1704.

Bedford, Arthur. *Serious Reflections on the Scandalous Abuse and Effects of the Stage: In a Sermon Preached at the Parish Church of St Nicholas in the City of Bristol, on Sunday, the 7th Day of January, 1704/5*. 1705.

Bedford, Arthur. *The Evil and Danger of Stage Plays: Showing their Natural Tendency to Destroy Religion, and Introduce a General Corruption of Manners; In Almost Two Thousand Instances, Taken from the Plays of the Two Last Years, Against All the Methods Lately Used for their Reformation*. 1706.

Dennis, John. *An Essay on The Operas After the Italian Manner, Which Are About to be Established on the English Stage: With Some Reflections on the Damage Which They May Bring to the Public*. 1706.

Filmer, Edward. *A Defence of Plays: Or the Stage Vindicated, from Several Passages in Mr Collier's* Short View, *etc. Wherein Is Offered the Most Probable Method of Reforming Our Plays. With a Consideration How Far Vicious Characters May Be Allowed on the Stage*. 1707.

Collier, Jeremy. *A Farther Vindication of the* Short View *of the Profaneness and Immorality of the English Stage. In which the Objections of a late Book entitled* A Defence of Plays, *are Considered*. 1708.

D'Urfey, Thomas. *The Old Mode and the New*. 1709.

Cibber, Colley. *The Non-Juror*. 1718.

Anonymous. *The Theatre-Royal Turned into a Mountebank's Stage. In Some Remarks Upon Mr Cibber's Quack-Dramatical Performance, Called* The Non-juror. 1718.

Law, William. *The Absolute Unlawfulness of the Stage-Entertainment Fully Demonstrated*. 1726.

BIBLIOGRAPHY

Anonymous. *Law Outlawed: or, A Short Reply to Mr Law's Long Declamation Against the Stage. Wherein the Wild Rant, Blind Passion, and False Reasoning of that Piping-hot Pharisee Are Made Apparent to the Meanest Capacity. Together with an Humble Petition to the Governors of the Incurable Ward of Bethlehem to Take Pity on the Poor Distracted Authors of the Town, and Not Suffer Them to Terrify Mankind at This Rate. Written at the Request of the Orange-Women, and for the Public Good, by the Impartial Pen of Mrs S____ O____, a Lover of Both Houses.* 1726.

Dennis, John. *The Stage Defended, From Scripture, Reason, Experience, and the Common Sense of Mankind, for Two Thousand Years. Occasioned by Mr Law's late Pamphlet against Stage-Entertainments.* 1726.

General

Anthony, Sister Rose. *The Jeremy Collier Stage Controversy 1698-1726.* Marquette University Press, Milwaukee 1937.

Banham, Martin (Editor). *The Cambridge Guide to Theatre.* Cambridge 1988, 1992.

Bateson, F. W. *Cambridge Bibliography of English Literature Vol. II.* Cambridge 1940.

Broxap, Henry. *The Later Non-jurors.* Cambridge, 1924.

Collins, P.A.W. *Restoration Comedy.* In: *The Pelican Guide to English Literature Vol. IV,* edited by Boris Ford. Pelican, 1957.

Craik, T. W. (Editor). *The Revels History of Drama in English. Vol. V.* Methuen, 1976.

Dobrée, Bonamy. *Restoration Comedy 1660-1720.* Oxford 1924.

Dobrée, Bonamy. *Restoration Tragedy 1660-1720.* Oxford 1929.

Dobrée, Bonamy (Editor). *The Complete Works of Sir John Vanbrugh.* Bloomsbury 1928.

Findlater, Richard. *Banned! - A Review of Theatrical Censorship in Britain.* MacGibbon and Kee, 1967.

Gray, I. E. and Potter, W. E. *Ipswich School 1400-1950.* Harrison and Sons, 1950.

Hughes, Geoffrey. *Swearing: A Social History of Foul Language, Oaths and Profanity in English.* Blackwell, 1991 and Penguin 1998.

Johnson, Samuel. *A Life of Congreve.* 1779-81.

Krutch, Joseph Wood. *Comedy and Conscience after the Restoration.* Columbia University Press, 1924 and 1949.

Legg, Wickham. *English Church Life.*

Nicholl, Allardyce. *A History of English Drama 1660-1900. Vol. I Restoration Drama.* Cambridge, 1952.

Partridge, Eric (abridged by Jacqueline Simpson). *A Dictionary of Historical Slang.* Penguin 1972.

Pepys, Samuel. *Diaries.* Various editions.

Sackville-West, Vita. *Knole and the Sackvilles.* Ernest Benn, 1922. New edition: National Trust, 1991.

Sampson, George. *Cambridge History of English Literature. Vols. VIII and IX.* Cambridge 1908.

Spingarn, J. E. *Critical Essays of the Seventeenth Century (Three volumes).* Oxford 1908.

Thomas, David (Editor, with Hare, Arnold). *Restoration and Georgian England 1660-1788* - In *Theatre in Europe: A Documentary History.* Cambridge 1989.

Venn, John. *Biographical History of Gonville and Caius College 1349-1897.* Cambridge, 1897.

Index

BIBLIOGRAPHY

Drama in the Cathedral

The Twentieth Century Encounter of Church and Stage

Kenneth Pickering

At the start of the twentieth century, dramatists often struggled to express the relevance of Christianity in the face of hostility from the established church. During the 1920s, the remarkable Dean of Canterbury Cathedral encouraged the use of dramatic verse to spread the Christian message. This impetus spread from the cathedral cities of Britain to all parts of the English-speaking world.

This radical return to earlier traditions, which included Eliot's *Murder in the Cathedral*, had its origins in changes of attitude, revivals of medieval drama and revolutionary ideas of staging. The extraordinary events charted in *Drama in the Cathedral* have often escaped the notice of other theatre historians and, combined with insights into the theological and social landscape of the times, provide an unique record of one of the most significant changes in the modern stage. To mark his appearance as Becket in a major new production of *Murder in the Cathedral*, the author has thoroughly up-dated the original edition to include productions and events from the latter half of the century.

***

KENNETH PICKERING turned from a successful teaching career to acting, writing and directing plays. His writing extends from rock musicals to religious plays and theatre textbooks. He is regarded as Britain's leading director of medieval drama following his massive productions of Mystery plays in Birmingham and Canterbury Cathedrals and Malvern and Tewkesbury Abbeys. He was recently Professor of Theatre at *Gonzaga University*, USA and is currently the Chief Examiner in Speech and Drama for the *London College of Music and Media*.

"There ought to be a book on this subject and you won't get a better one." -
Peter Levi on the First Edition.

***

ISBN: 0 85343 627 4 - Second Edition
J. Garnet Miller

Saints and Their Emblems

Robert Milburn

Each figure of a saint in a church, whether in stone, glass or wood, depicts a particular person, but they are rarely named, so the interested visitor is dependent on guidebooks to identify them. St George and a few others are well-known, but in medieval times images were often used to convey identity, so many other saints were given an emblem or object as a common identifier.

This book lists over 250 saints, including all the common saints and many uncommon ones, each of whom is connected with at least one English church. The author gives a brief history of the saint in fact or legend and describes the identifying emblem. The commonest emblems are illustrated by small drawings.

Robert Milburn was an Honorary Fellow of Worcester College, Oxford and was Dean of Worcester from 1957-1968. His other works include *Early Christian Interpretations of History* and *Early Christian Art and Architecture*.

ISBN: 0 85956 064 3

Cressrelles Publishing Company

These titles, plus a wide range of plays for all theatres (children's, mixed and all-women) including religious plays, and theatre textbooks can be obtained from:

Cressrelles Publishing Company Limited
10 Station Road Industrial Estate, Colwall,
Near Malvern, WR13 6RN
Telephone/Fax: (01684) 540154